"Fantastic, Intelligent, Practical, Sensible, Fun—Annual Reports without fear!"

Sarah Nuttall—Noted B2B Copywriter, United Kingdom

"Corporate Communications and Investor Relations professionals everywhere will find their annual reporting duties simplified and their results more impactful by this detailed and insightful guide. Roth's ideas will benefit not only the writers of annual reports, but the shareholders, analysts and regulators whose fortunes depend on reading them.

David Laufer—Executive Vice President, Creative Services
Dynamic Marketing Systems;
Past President of NIRI-Atlanta chapter

"Robert Roth's book does a brilliant job of describing the process from the vantage of a journeyman annual report writer. This tool will be invaluable to both writers and designers long into the future. Thanks for the story well told Robert.

Jon Franz—Senior Creative Manager, MARCOM
Kimberley-Clark

"I wouldn't venture down the annual report path without a copy of the Writer's Guide firmly in my grasp."

Nancy Chase, Ph.D.—Georgia State University
Department of English

# The Writer's Guide
to
# Annual Reports

# The Writer's Guide
## to
# Annual Reports

## Robert Roth

*To my wife, Danna*

# Contents

# Acknowledgments

While my name is on the front cover, I could not have authored this book without the generous help and contributions of friends and colleagues.

To my good friend (and crack proofreader) Jan Barstow, thank you for your support and unerring sense of what is right. Thanks, also, to Deborah Pinals, Esther Kim and Rob Truetel at Critt Graham + Associates, for the great cover design. Thanks also to Kathi Roberts of Roberts Design for her valuable design wisdom and to Terry Davis for all of her encouragement.

A huge thank-you to the folks at see see eye — Jeanie Flohr Treadaway, Lawson Cox, Rodolfo Ruiz Sosa and Teresa Wheeler — for helping with CVS Caremark, Goodrich Corporation and Crawford & Company. Likewise to Gretel Going at Channel V Media and Sun McElderry at Story Worldwide for helping with Bank of America. Thanks also to Don Mitchell at Mindpower for his assistance and Jean Ann Jedwabny-Almus for the scans.

On the corporate side, thanks go to Donna Sitkiewicz at Kraft Foods, Irene Kisleiko at Quaker Chemical, Kara Pardini at Crawford & Company, Katie A. Reinsmidt at CBL & Associates Properties, Terri Cohilas Kundert at Southern Company, Bill McCarthy at Neenah Paper, John-Paul Schuirink at Sara Lee Corporation, Mike McGuire at CVS Caremark, and Lisa Bottle at Goodrich Corporation for making the Annual Reports Gallery possible.

I would also like to express special appreciation to Martin Flaherty at pencil box, Chuck Reese at Chuck Reese Communications and Steve Beshara at Vista for their constructive ideas.

And finally, to Rick Anwyl, thanks for showing me the way.

# Foreword

## Caution!

A twisted perilous road is the writer's path to clarity and believability.

Begin. Stop. Is this important? More research, too much information, another interview, another meeting, confirm, dispute, rewrite. What is the point? Is there a point? Too short. Where do I stop? Define voice, tone, organization, style, acronyms, synonyms, adverbs and adjectives. Headlines, taglines, more words, fewer words. Is less really more?

If this does not resonate, and if you are embarking on writing a company's annual report, it shall all make sense shortly. The good news – help is in your hands.

## Finally

This book has so long been needed; it will quickly become a staple on the desk wherever annual reports are produced. Within, you will find the writer's role outlined, the fundamental steps in the annual report writing process and definitions of process components, along with key distinctions in terminology. You will find pearls of wisdom, tips, clues and the warnings only a well-informed and seasoned professional could provide. View it as a guide, a tutorial; whether virgin or veteran, freelance writer, graphic designer or part of a corporate team charged with annual report development, you will quickly find it an invaluable resource tool.

## Context

The role of the annual report has expanded well beyond simply reporting financial data and historical information. Today's annual report is widely regarded as one of the single most valuable strategic communication tools at a company's disposal. It has become a primary platform for evolving and disseminating essential corporate messaging to a broadening host of constituents.

Further, informed communications professionals acknowledge that the development process itself is now viewed as an important management tool for advancing, refining and evaluating thinking on key corporate initiatives. This process surfaces and distills thought and messages on such central topics as social and environmental responsibility, corporate vision and mission, strategic direction, leadership, marketplace dynamics, competitive landscape and more, as well as producing an annual report card on corporate performance against goals and objectives.

## The Fundamental Need

At its core, development of an annual report revolves around the need for today's publicly held corporations to clearly define and express valuable messages to its owners (shareholders). Beyond this primary audience, the annual report has assumed a vital role in communicating with employees, customers, governments, the industry and the world at large. It has become the principal vehicle through which a corporation communicates who it is, what it represents and stands for, what activities it is engaged in, and why, what it has achieved and what it intends to accomplish next.

## The Writer's Challenge

Many of today's publicly owned corporations are vast and complex organizations with varied operating structures. They are comprised of senior management teams, marketing groups, human resource departments, finance and legal departments, communications and public affairs departments, as well as numerous product and service groups operating both domestically and in foreign countries. They may have strategic partnerships, licensing agreements, contracts with institutions, corporations and governments. Each of these desires a voice, with its contributions and achievements included and portrayed correctly in the company's annual report.

The challenge of telling their stories, distilling these varied needs and perspectives to an accurate, compelling, memorable and unified communication ultimately falls to the writer's shoulders. I have long believed that good annual report writing makes for okay reading. Great annual report writing creates exponential value and differentiation. Great writing can empower a culture, alter perception, spark innovation, shift battlegrounds, expunge doubt and define the future. As a writer of annual reports, your challenge is to move from good to great. This book will show you how.

Rick Anwyl
The Center for Design Study
Atlanta, Georgia

# Introduction

## What This Book Is About

Let's start with what this book is not about. It's not about how to read and analyze the financial information that you'll find in a typical annual report. Nor does it deal with annual report production issues, like choosing an appropriate typeface, paper weight or color palette. Nor does it provide handy checklists with breezy titles like "10 Good Themes for Your Next Annual Report."

What this book does, instead, is help you create and write an annual report. More specifically, it helps you write an annual report that other people might actually want to read.

This book guides you through the concept and writing stages of narrative development—covering everything from development of the key message to the final version of the copy. The approach it offers is based on the same creative process I've used successfully for more than twenty years as a professional copywriter.

If you're involved in writing, designing and/or producing annual reports—either freelance or in-house—this book can do three things for you:

- It can help you think more strategically about your annual report
- It can kick-start your creative thinking.
- It can strengthen your writing skills.

I have used simple examples throughout the book so that it will be easier for you to understand the principles behind them. I don't mean them to be templates. They are points of departure. Utilizing your own creative thinking, you should be able to do far better than I did.

*Chapter One*

# The Players

## Welcome to the Team

When creating an annual report, keep in mind the old adage, "Two heads are better than one." As the writer, your second head will most likely be the designer. Together you form the annual report team.

## Defining the Annual Report's Role

The SEC (U.S. Securities and Exchange Commission) defines the typical annual report to shareholders as a "state-of-the-company report," which they say includes "an opening letter from the Chief Executive Officer, financial data, results of continuing operations, market segment information, new product plans, subsidiary activities, and research and development activities on future programs."

Today, the role of the annual report has expanded beyond reporting financial data and historical information. It has a become a platform from which companies launch new products or marketing strategies, address behavioral or morale issues, or even alter strategic direction.

According to Rick Anwyl, founder of The Center of Design Studies and veteran of many IBM annual reports, an annual report should tell the story of what a company is doing; what it said it was going to do, what it actually did, and most importantly—what it intends to do next.

"The dynamics of that are caught up in the company's need to tell its owners (shareholders) everything that is going on," explains Rick. "The folks over in marketing want to be sure that they tell the whole story. Ditto for the people in manufacturing, management, human resources, legal, finance and community affairs. They all want to be absolutely certain that their story is told the right way."

Your job is to tell that story as a unified message within your annual report—one that begins on the front cover and ends on the back cover. This book shows you how to do that, how to develop the strategic message that drives the narrative story, how to communicate your company's or client's vision and direction, how to deliver content in a compelling and creative way.

## Defining the Writer's Role

Obviously, the writer's role is to write. But before that can happen, you first must lead the discovery, strategy and concept phases of annual report development. After that, you must choose what to write. In that regard, you'll act as "content cop" for the process.

There's more going on in the company than could fit between the covers of the annual report you are writing. Every department is clamoring for attention. That puts a lot of pressure on you to please everyone. Don't succumb to it. You'll end up writing too much. As a result, the company's key message will be diluted or worse yet, lost.

## Defining the Designer's Role

Unless you are that rare creative person who both writes and designs, you'll need a designer to help you develop and complete your annual report. The designer's role is not simply to "decorate" the annual report, but to be a strategic ally. Like Ginger Rogers and Fred Astaire, you'll work as a team. Together you'll drive the annual report's progress—each of you contributing ideas that shape its look, feel and communications message.

Some companies have in-house graphics capability, which means you'll work with one of their in-house designers on the annual report. Or you could be asked to bring in a freelance designer from the outside. If that's the case, save yourself some headaches by selecting a designer with prior annual report experience.

## Defining the Format

According to the SEC, reporting companies must send proxy materials and some type of "annual report" to their shareholders when they hold annual meetings to elect directors. Beyond that requirement, the design, content and production of the annual report is up to you—there are no standards.

Companies must also file a Form 10-K with the SEC. The 10-K typically contains more detailed information about the company's financial condition than the annual report. The 10-K is printed by specialized financial printing firms on lightweight newsprint. Companies can send a Form 10-K to shareholders in a lieu of an annual report, usually in the form of a "10-K Wrap." That's basically the pre-printed 10-K, wrapped in a front and back cover, a letter to the shareholders and maybe a short narrative.

The SEC is constantly massaging the rules that affect the delivery of annual reports, 10-K's, 10-K wraps and proxy materials to shareholders and potential investors. Electronic delivery of those elements is gaining acceptance and momentum. Will electronic media displace printed media the way the car displaced the horse? Probably not for a long while, which gives you ample time to write your annual report masterpiece.

## Chapter Two

# **Anatomy Lesson**

## **How Your Annual Report Fits Together**

There is no standard blueprint for how the elements of an annual report fit together. The following components, however, are common to many annual reports. As the writer, you will normally be involved with the front (or narrative) portion of the book, not the financials.

# Components of a Typical Annual Report

### Front Cover (FC)

The front cover of your annual report is prime territory. It's the place where your concept and message should begin. Properly executed, the front cover's job is to set the narrative tone and pull the reader inside the book.

### Inside Front Cover (IFC)

The inside front cover is generally reserved for Financial Highlights, Table of Contents, business description and/or company vision and mission. It can also be pressed into service as part of the narrative.

### Financial Highlights

This is an abridged comparative summary of financial performance and stock data for the year, usually presented in easy-to-read chart and/or table form near the front of the book.

### First Text Page

The first text page can play one of several roles: As a single page, it becomes the transitional element between the cover and the inside narrative. It can also serve as the starting page of the Letter to Shareholders. Or, used in conjunction with the inside front cover, it can create a spread (two facing pages used as one).

### Letter to Shareholders

The Letter to Shareholders is a critical part of the annual report, signed by the CEO (Chief Executive Officer), the Chairman or both. Some corporate communications folks go so far as to say (jokingly) that the Letter to Shareholders and the Financial Highlights are the only things people read. Let's hope not. Generally, the letter spans one or two spreads.

Although you are writing the narrative portion of the annual report, you may not be asked to draft the letter—that task varies from company to company.

## Narrative

From a writing standpoint, the narrative section is the heart of the annual report. This is where your story takes shape, governed by your key message. The length of the narrative varies, controlled mostly by budget, content and concept. The narrative can be built with spreads, single pages or a combination of both.

## Operational Review

This is an optional subset of the narrative, organized around operating divisions or segments. It's usually a separate section that reports on divisional performance, providing more detail than is found in the narrative. It's a good way of defining each division. Operational reviews are a good thing. Otherwise, you would have to cram all of those details into the narrative itself.

## Board of Directors

This section is not part of the narrative. It displays the company's board, singularly or as a group, along with pertinent information and the committees on which each serves. Most likely, if you are not an in-house writer, this is not something you will write

## Corporate Governance

The CFO or the Senior Executive Vice President generally writes the corporate governance section. Driven in part by the Sarbanes-Oxley

Act (SOx), this section covers processes, policies administrative controls and accountability measures the company has put in place.

## Financial Statement

In number of pages, the majority of the annual report is devoted to your company's or client's Financial Statement. Among other reports, this contains a balance sheet (assets and liabilities), an income statement, a cash flow statement and a statement of retained earnings. This section is the exclusive domain of the financial folks.

## Management Discussion & Analysis

Also included in the Financial Statement is the Management Discussion & Analysis or MD&A. The information in the MD&A provides investors with a clearer picture of the how the company fared in the previous year. C-level management writes this section.

## At-a-Glance

At-a-glance is a spread, multi-spread or single-page snapshot of the company (often in the form of charts and tables) that shows products, markets, geographies and other pertinent company information—in other words, how the corporation fits together. Investors and analysts are fond of ripping at-a-glance sections out of the annual reports and filing them (or so I've been told).

## Inside Back Cover (IBC)

The inside back cover is mostly used for listing company locations and shareholder information.

## Back Cover (BC)

Think of this as underutilized space. The BC is the perfect place to end your concept with a poetic "punctuation" mark.

*Chapter Three*

# The Annual Report Process

## A Work In Progress

No matter how many annual reports I write, for me, the annual report process remains a work in progress, reflective not just of my own ongoing experiences, but that of the smart communications professionals I've been lucky enough to work with over the past 20 years.

Of course, your approach to a communications project may differ from mine. So you don't need to feel shackled to the entire process presented in this book to benefit from it. Just take the parts you find helpful and leave the rest on the table.

## The Annual Report Process

| | |
|---|---|
| 1. DISCOVERY | Just as in the legal context, discovery is the act of obtaining relevant information—in your case, about the company or organization whose annual report you are writing. |
| 2. KEY MESSAGE | The key message is the strategic foundation for the annual report. You cannot develop concepts or copy without first determining what your key message is. |
| 3. CONCEPT DEVELOPMENT | It's time to exercise your right brain, as your thinking moves from strategic to creative. Concepts are rooted in your key message. In fact, concepts are the creative expression of that message. You can develop more than one concept for the same message. As you begin the concept development phase, shoot for at least three different ideas. |
| 4. COPY OUTLINE | After your concept is approved by the powers to be, the next step is to develop a copy outline. The outline is the framework that supports the copy. It normally lists headlines, subheads and bulleted copy points for every page or spread. |
| 5. FIRST DRAFT | This is where you get down to the business of writing. The copywriting phase brings your copy outline to life. Expect to make at least three revisions to the narrative. Most of the time, it's more. |
| 6. REVISIONS | Revisions come in two sizes: minor and major. Most annual report projects include some of each. The good news: This is the last step. |

## Keep the Committee in the Loop

No matter how much you'd like to fly solo on your annual report, it's not going to happen. Most organizations have an internal communications committee that reviews and approves each phase of the annual report's development, from concept to final copy. The committee's buy-in is essential in selling the annual report to C-level management.

If you're fortunate, your review committee will act as a helpful part of your team. They will make suggestions about the copy and design rather than dictate changes. However, if they do dictate, you'll need to find a way to incorporate their changes while maintaining a pleasant attitude. It should come as no surprise that in the end, the committee is always right.

*Chapter Four*

# Discovery

One caveat before we start. There's a tendency to minimize the importance of Discovery, especially if you are already familiar with the company or industry about which you're writing. Resist the temptation to see things that way and try to view your company or client with new eyes.

## Make a Binder

Writing an annual report means juggling a lot of information. Nothing beats a three-ring binder for helping you organize it. We're not talking about anything fancy here—you can even use write-on tabs to divide the sections.

Section titles might include:

- 10-K
- Speeches
- Quarterly reports
- Concepts/Ideas/Themes
- Copy outline
- Interviews
- Vision
- Initiatives
- Analysts
- Case studies
- Previous AR
- PowerPoint(s)

Organize your binder any way you wish, but the point is: Make sure you have one.

### Gather Existing Materials

Most of the information you need already exists somewhere else. All you have to do is find and capture it. And you should capture as much of it as possible, as your findings will influence your key message and creative concepts. Here are some suggested items that should go into your three-ring binder:

### The Previous Year's Annual Report

The events and messaging in annual reports tend to overlap from one year to another, forming a continuum of a company's activities.

For consistency's sake, begin your discovery with the previous year's annual report.

## Form 10-K (selected portions)

The previous year's Form 10-K, which your company or client filed with the SEC, can reveal some interesting background facts. It can also provide a new perspective on the competitive factors affecting their business. The 10-K is a good a place to ground yourself in your company's business and get a generalized overview. Keep in mind, though, it's a year behind the point from which you are now starting.

## Speeches

Speeches made throughout the year by the CEO and/or Chairman yield not only the language and tone of the company, but just as important, its direction. Focus on the consistent messages that occur from speech to speech and ignore any disconnects.

## Road Show

The "road show" is the PowerPoint presentation that the CEO and investor relations (IR) folks present to analysts, investors and institutional groups. It provides a current snapshot of the industry, the problems and opportunities facing your Company, and where your Company is headed strategically. Make sure you get the latest, greatest version.

## Other Presentations

These include other PowerPoint presentations or speeches that companies make to analysts, shareholders, employees, retirees and community leaders throughout the year.

## Quarterly Reports

Publicly traded companies are required to file quarterly performance reports (Form 10-Q) with the SEC. They also distribute that information as a financial news release and post it on the company's Web site.

## Press or News Releases

In addition to financial news releases, companies issue press releases on a variety of subjects ranging from community relations and industry recognition to new product launches and newly hired executives. Print out the relevant ones or, if the list of press releases is extensive, print out a chronological list of the headings. You can use that as a guide to find what you want later on.

## Earnings Calls

These are transcripts or recordings of the company's quarterly conference call releases of financial data including revenue and earnings. Analysts who follow the stock can call in to ask questions.

## Company HR Magazine

If your company's employee magazine deals with corporate, strategic or behavioral issues, it can provide useful insights.

## Product, Service or Capability Brochures

These are essential if new products or services will be part of your narrative story. One caveat: Don't get lost in the details.

## Web Search

Anything goes in this regard. Search mainly for competitive information, industry information and external views of your company or nonprofit organization.

## Analyst Reports

Analysts who work for brokerage firms track companies' performance and issue evaluative reports. These reports can provide an insightful, outside point of view.

## Competitive Annual Reports

A competitive review can be helpful when starting a new annual report project. Compare last year's annual report to that of your top competitors. Focus more on the messaging than the design. Did you deliver your key message in a clear, compelling way? How well did your competitors deliver theirs?

## Interviews

Last on this list but first in importance. Interviews with key executives, whether face to face or over the telephone, are critical to the success of the annual report process. What you'll learn by talking to the CEO and other top-ranking executives will help set the narrative's direction and provide the proper filter for all the materials and information you've unearthed during the discovery phase.

## Develop a Questionnaire

The first rule of interviewing is never shoot from the hip. Develop a written questionnaire and provide it to interviewees several days in advance. That gives everyone enough time to frame his or her answers. Remember, you're not from *60 Minutes*, so the questions should not put people on the spot. Instead, they should function as starting points to a broader conversation about the company. Treat them as topics for exploration.

What are some of the questions you should ask? The following is an example based on various questionnaires that I use. In its current state, the questionnaire is too long. So, consider it a starting point. Use it as a guide for creating your own questionnaire. Revise and/or add and subtract to it as you see fit.

What you want to nail down in your interviews are the challenges and opportunities your company faces, the initiatives launched, its overall performance and, most importantly, the overarching message to convey.

**TIPS:**

1. To keep your interviewees engaged, don't let the interview run over 45 minutes.
2. Ask open-ended questions whenever possible. (Questions that can't be answered with yes or no.)
3. Record your interviews on tape or digital media and have them transcribed.

# Sample Annual Report Questions

## Challenges and opportunities

- What are the major success stories from last year?
- What are some of the major challenges and opportunities (Company) now faces
- What new initiatives and/or partnerships should be discussed in this annual report?

## Innovation

- What new products or technology should be included in this annual report?

## Growth

- What will drive sustained new growth for (Company)?

## Performance

- How would you describe (Company's) financial performance the past year?

## Culture

- What stands out most about (Company's) culture?

## The environment

- What environmental issues are important to (Company)? What are you doing about them?

## Efficiency

- How is (Company) enhancing efficiency?

## Customer service

- What new customer service initiatives did (Company) launch in the past year?

## Company-specific question(s)

- Do your homework and ask one or two topical questions relating directly to (Company).

## Messaging

- What could this annual report make clearer to your audiences?
- If stakeholders could only remember one thing about (Company) after reading the annual report, what should that be?
- What did you like/dislike about your prior year's annual report?

## Outlook

- What excites you most about (Company's) future?

## Wrap-up

- Have I left something out?

*Chapter Five*

# Determining the Key Message

It would be terrific if you could dump all of your findings and interviews into the hopper of some big machine, push a button, and out would pop the key message your annual report should deliver. Unfortunately, there isn't such a machine, which means you have to do the work yourself.

## The Key Message Says It All

Our mission here is to develop a key message for the annual report. Before getting started, however, let's review what a key message is. As described earlier, the key message is strategic, not creative. It is the foundation for the concept and content of your annual report. Think of the key message as everything you learned in discovery boiled down to its essence—one or two sentences that define (Company's) point of view for this annual report.

Here are four examples of key messages taken from actual communications briefs:

1. **Company A's realistic approach to managing its business enables it to make smart decisions about its future.**
2. **No matter how buyer and seller connect, Company B adds the essential component that lets commerce happen.**
3. **As a sophisticated and successful owner, developer and manager of market-dominant properties in middle market locations, Company C is in the right position to attract more retailers.**
4. **Credibility, Discipline and Confidence—Company D is taking an intelligent, well-managed approach to growth and will continue to prove it can deliver what it promises.**

The key message isn't a permanent message. It changes from year to year, in accordance with your company's strategic direction. Don't confuse the key message with a tag line, positioning line or brand promise. It is none of those. Nor is it a creative idea or theme. The key message is simply an articulation of your Company's positioning relative to the particular annual report you are writing. Nonetheless, its effect on the creative development of your annual report is profound, as the key message must support the weight of the narrative.

## Analysis of Findings

How do you develop your key message? Start by analyzing your findings. In this step, you take all of the information you unearthed during the discovery process and begin to make sense of it. A good way to do that is to pare it down into a simple two-columned chart. You can draw the chart freehand, or set up it up as a two-columned table in a WORD® document. Label the left-hand column PAST/PRESENT. Label the right-hand column FUTURE. Now go through your findings, notes, interviews, etc.; pick out the relevant points and put them on the appropriate side of your chart.

Why should you do this? Four reasons:

A. It organizes your findings, providing greater insight into your content.
B. It helps you identify the elements of your key message.
C. It gives you a realistic sense of where your company is, in relation to where it's headed
D. It provides a framework for concept development and writing the copy outline.

## Creating the Chart

What kind of information should you include in your chart? Here are some categories to guide you. The list is by no means inclusive, so add whatever you think is relevant.

You're looking for golden nuggets—snippets of information, statements from key executives, analysts' comments, and most important, your own take on the situation. The chart does not read across the rows. Each column is independent of the other.

# Categories of Information

## Past/Present

- Mission-related statements
- Financial performance

- Initiatives launched
- Challenges met
- Acquisitions
- Achievements for the year
- Awards & industry recognition
- Competitive pressures
- Core value statements
- Diversity statements
- Industry events/trends
- Market events/trends
- Community affairs
- Environmental issues
- Etc.

## Future

- Vision
- Opportunities
- New challenges
- New markets
- New products
- Corporate culture
- New technology
- New initiatives
- Growth strategy
- Leadership
- Industry events/trends
- Market events/trends
- Etc.

## Not for profit

If you're writing for a nonprofit organization, use the listed categories that apply and add the following new categories:

- Accomplishments
- Fundraising

- Contributions
- Community partners
- Balance sheet

## Developing Your Key Message

Once your chart is complete, you're ready to develop your key message. Keep in mind that you're not creating a theme or concept at this point. You're simply composing a one- or two-sentence statement that defines your company in a unique way for the annual report. The key message should enlighten in a way that adds value to your corporate brand—in other words, in a way that differentiates your company from others in your industry.

When writing the key message, avoid dull, vague statements like "As global leader in widgets, we will continue to be a global leader in widgets." Drill down. The more specific you can be, the stronger your message becomes. "As a global leader in widgets, we're not about to rest. We launched a five-year, strategic growth plan that will ensure our continued dominance of the marketplace."

The key message must sound believable. And interesting. It should define your company in a unique way, establishing a relationship between where your company is now and where it's going. The trick is to come up with a set of words that not only defines your company's uniqueness, but also is capable of supporting the creative concept you'll develop in the next step.

Study the four key message examples presented earlier in this chapter. Each positions the company in a way that is both clear and unique. Everything about the annual report—concept, headlines, copy, images and design—should, in some way, link back to the key mesage.

As with everything else involved with bringing an annual report to life, there is no right or wrong way to develop a key message. Nonetheless, here are some suggested methods for going about it:

## Word or Phrase Patterns

Once you complete your two-column list, look for words or phrases that appear with regularity throughout your findings. In Company A's case, the word "realistic" appeared over and over in everything from speeches to press releases to internal communications. It quickly became the substance of the key message.

## Ideas

Identify the big ideas that drove the Company's achievements during the year. Was it a focus on organic growth? Innovation? Quality initiatives?

## Positioning

Where is the company in the marketplace? Where is it headed? What drives it? This is the approach Company B and Company C used.

## Stories

What kind of a story will your findings support? A growth story? A competitive story? A success story? An innovation story? A longevity story?

## Mission/Vision

Do your findings support the company's mission or vision? If so, in what way? Company D's key message reflects this approach.

## Divining

Don't laugh—this is a field-tested way to determine your key message. Spread out your information on your desk and study it quietly. If you made a chart, slowly read each entry on it. If you didn't make a chart, look through your notes or binder. Ultimately, something will come to you. It always does.

## You're Not Finished Yet

Technically, your key message is not the end of the strategic thinking process. The communications brief is. It's a strategy document used in advertising, marketing communications and corporate com-munications. It's called a brief because it's supposed to be brief.

The brief boils down everything you need to know to create an annual report concept into one or two pages. You can find a variety of templates for creative briefs online. But all you need to know is the answers to five questions (most of which you've already learned in the Discovery phase).

## A Brief Communications Brief:

### 1) Who are we talking to?

List the different audiences for this annual report

### 2) What do they believe about (Company) now?

Write down what each audience presently thinks about (Company) and its performance, e.g., they might think that (Company's) growth is slowing or that competitive pressure is increasing.

### 3) What do we want them to believe?

Whatever they believe now is their reality. Your job is to give them something better to believe, e.g., (Company has in place the elements it needs to accelerate growth

### 4) What is our key message?

Insert (Company's) key message here.

### 5) What is the support for that message?

Write five or more supporting points (bullets are fine) that serve as proof of your key message.

## Get Approval

Everyone on the annual report team must sign off on the communications brief before you can use it. If you jump the gun, you can leave yourself open to plenty of extra do-over work.

*Chapter Six*

# Thinking Creatively

Up to now, you've been using the left side of your brain to strategize and organize. Now it's time to switch to the right side and come up with a creative concept for your annual report.

What is a concept? For our purposes, it's the creative expression of the key message—an intriguing idea that will capture your audience's attention.

## Concept or Theme?

To me, there is a difference between a theme and a concept. Themes don't make readers think, or at least, don't make them think very hard. Themes are more about motif and decoration than ideas. Thematic elements lend themselves well to metaphors, such as the use of mountain-climbing images to represent achievement, growth, vision or obstacles overcome.

In developing your annual report, you should always strive for concepts first.

Concepts are brainier than themes. They are ideas inferred directly from the key message itself. Concepts are more strategic than themes. Concepts can exist without images. They can be clever, smart, humorous, unexpected and attention grabbing.

Here's an example of a simple concept for a pharmaceutical company. We'll name the concept "Point of View:"

*Front cover:*
**Seeing Is Believing**

*Intro copy:*
**At (Company), we believe that how you perceive physicians, patients, competition and the academic community has a lot to do with success. Actually, it has everything to do with *our* success.**

*Headline examples:*
- **Keeping a tight focus on product leadership**
- **Broadening our view of physicians' practices.**
- **Looking beyond the business of today.**

## Let's Get Creative—Part 1

There's no right or wrong method for developing a creative concept—all you need is the right inspiration. And one of the best ways to get it and jumpstart the creative side of your brain is to review what others have created.

You'll find plenty to look at in the latest edition of the *AR100* book, published annually by Black Book. In addition, you can download copies of annual reports from Buckminister.com (for a slight fee). Finally, most companies post a PDF or HTML version of their last two annual reports on their Web sites.

You should also build your own annual report library. You can order free annual reports by the boxload from Annual Report Service and The Public Register's Annual Report Service online. Or just do a Web search using the term "Free Annual Reports."

Don't limit yourself to just annual reports from your industry. Good ideas are good ideas, wherever you may find them.

## Let's Get Creative—Part 2

Okay—you've looked at other people's work. Now it's time to come up with your own creative ideas. To get your creative juices flowing, try one or more of the following creative exercises. You'll use these exercises in the next chapter, "Developing a Concept."

## Make a Word List

Developing a word list is a good way to stimulate creative thinking. More than just an exercise, the list of words you construct can help you when creating your concept.

Here's how it works: With your key message in front of you, write down (or key in) every word that comes into your mind. If you have the space, use large easel paper so you can stick your word lists up on the walls.

Don't prejudge. Write down all the words that pop into your head, even those that don't make sense or seem way off target.

Next, play with the words. Try combining a few of them. Add some synonyms to the list. Use one or two words in a phrase. Do words on your list suggest other words? Write them down, also.

Next, narrow your word list down. Which words on your list best link up to your key message? Put them on a separate list.

## Sleep on It

This is a very useful method for solving problems—creative or otherwise. Known as "unconscious problem solving," it consists of feeding your mind a problem to solve just before you go to sleep.

Psychologists call that incubation. You can think about the problem or just read your notes. When you awaken the next morning, your mind magically has an answer.

It's a good idea to keep a pen and small pad of paper next to your bed. Sometimes the answer comes in the middle of the night, and unless you write it down, you won't remember it. Promise.

## Daydream

Pretend you have ADD (Attention Deficit Disorder). Let your mind wander. Your subconscious will do the heavy lifting.

## Ask Why

Think of your company as a big red onion. Asking "Why?" is a great way to peel back the layers and get to some inner truths. Police detectives ask *why?* a lot.

## Brainstorm

It's best to limit participation to you, the designer, the corporate communications director and maybe someone from investor relations, although you can add as many cast members as you want. Lock yourselves in a conference room and start brainstorming. Everyone throws out creative ideas in rapid-fire succession. Someone writes it all down on an easel pad.

There's one rule: no discussing or analyzing the ideas until the brainstorming session is over. Sometimes it pays to let the ideas cook overnight before you evaluate them.

The brainstorming context should be creative, playful, imaginative and fun. Don't criticize or judge, no matter how lame the idea sounds to you.

*Chapter Seven*

# Developing a Concept

OK, you've developed a key message; you've done some creative thinking, now it's time to pull it all together into a creative concept. Actually, you should shoot for three separate concepts for your annual report. The folks on the annual report approval committee always appreciate (read: expect) a choice.

## Start on the Front Cover

One of the best places to begin creative development for your annual report is on the front cover. After all, that's the first thing your readers will see. Your job is to get them past the cover and into the narrative. What follows in this chapter are some conceptual approaches to help you accomplish that.

TIP: Begin with the key message—again. Always start each creative session by taping your key message to the wall. That way, you won't venture too far off course.

## **Approach 1:** Set Up a Reveal on the Cover

In French cooking, many recipes begin with the instruction: "Make a roux" (butter and flour cooked together). In creating annual reports, we often begin with the phrase: "Make a reveal."

What is a "reveal?" If you've ever read a humorous greeting card, then you've experienced a reveal. The format is generally the same: a setup on the cover—a question or something that piques the reader's curiosity or is intriguing—followed by a strategic payoff (the reveal) on the first text page inside.

**How does a "reveal" work in the context of an annual report? Some examples follow.**

## *Reveal Example 1:* *A Regional Power Company*

### Situation:

A regional power company was expanding into new forms of energy. They needed a way to tell that story to investors.

### Front Cover:

On the cover of their annual report was the phrase,
"A word about our future."

### Reveal Page:

The payoff is on the first text page, a single bold word, "Energy."

## **Reveal Example 2:** A Global Paper Company

### Situation:

This paper company was spun off by its giant corporate parent. This annual report was their first. As an Initial Public Offering (IPO), the new company needed a way to introduce itself to a variety of stakeholders—institutional investors, retail investors, analysts and employees.

### Front Cover:

The cover of the annual report posed the question, ***"How do you make a great first impression?"***

### Intro Page:

The answer takes the form of a simple imperative sentence: "***Start with a blank sheet of paper.***"
**Note:** Posing a question on the cover of your annual report is a popular way to create a reveal. A question piques readers' curiosity—hopefully enough to cause them to open the book for the answer.

## *Reveal Example 3:* An Orthodontic Technology Company

### Situation:

Many investors simply scan the annual report, immune to the words that you so painstakingly write. This company found a way around that—building their three-part message into the reveal itself.

### Front Cover:

The front cover proclaims, "***The evidence is clear.***" Beneath that is an off-center image of a smiling woman. Why is she smiling? You have to open the cover to find out.

### Intro Page:

The payoff line is, "***We're getting results.***" Listed under that are the three major accomplishments for the year, each with some brief explanatory copy:
   ***Our business model is working.***
   ***We're creating opportunities for orthodontists and dentists***
   ***Our product applications continue to grow.***

**Note:** If you read nothing else but the cover and the first text page, you come away with a good understanding of the company's performance.

## **Reveal Example 4:** An Engineered Products Company

### Situation:

(Company) had a record year and sought a way to explain the positive factors that drove their success.

**Front Cover:**

The cover poses a simple question, *"**What counts?**"*

**Intro Page:**

Text page one provides the answer: *"**Markets, Customers, Leadership, Discipline, Cash, Results**"*

**Note:** This multi-part answer segues easily into a discussion of these qualities (one per page).

# **Approach 2:** Use a Single Word or Phrase on the Cover

If you feel a reveal is not right for your key message, consider using a word or short phrase on the front cover. Of course, the more you are able to link that word or phrase to your company's key message, mission, vision or performance—the better.

Select a word or phrase that supports your concept and has meaning to a wide audience. Think of your mother (who might also be a stockholder). Would she be able to understand the word or phrase you are using?

Avoid using company or industry jargon. You're looking for a simple word or phrase that communicates part of your message, a word that can become the foundation for the narrative that follows.

What sort of words are these? See the examples that follow. This is by no means an inclusive list. Use it to launch your own creative thinking.

## Sample Cover Words & Phrases

A New Way
A Step Above
A Step Ahead
Acceleration
Access
Always
Beyond the Horizon
Coming Together
Competitive
Delivering on Our Promises
Delivering Value
Envision
Everyday Matters
Evolution
Excellence
Fast
Focusing on _____
Gaining momentum
Gathering speed
Giant Steps
Growth
Higher Ground
Impressive
In a Perfect World
Innovation
Integration
Into Action
Investing in Success
Leadership
Leading the Way
Mileposts
Momentum
More
Navigating for success

New _____
New Directions
New Frontiers
New Horizons
On Top
Opportunity
Our Journey Continues
Pedal to the Metal
Playing to Win
Positioned for _____
Promises Kept
Quality
Redefining
Refocusing on Fundamentals
Signposts
Soaring
Strength
Support
The Next Chapter of Growth
The Right Strategy
The Road Ahead
Together
Transformation
Values
Vision

## **Word on the Cover Example 1:** A Prescription Drug Delivery Company

### Situation:

The company has a strong position in a rapidly expanding marketplace. They wanted this annual report to reflect their future opportunities.

### Front Cover:

The word that best characterized the company's position is *"**Opportunity**."* That word appears alone and embossed on the cover.

### Text Page 1:

When you open the book, you see the words *"**is everywhere**"*—which completes the phrase: *"**Opportunity is everywhere.**"* A small, bold block of introductory copy is printed beneath that phrase:

*"**Everywhere we look, we see opportunity. A burgeoning biopharmaceutical pipeline. An increasing focus on clinical excellence and support. A growing demand for high-touch and high-tech healthcare solutions. Ours is an evolving marketplace where infrastructure, experience and innovation are keys to success. The opportunities are endless. And no company is in a better position to leverage all of these opportunities than ours.**"*

**Note:** Most concepts, regardless of their construction, require some sort of introductory or explanatory copy. The usual place to stick it is on text page 1 (the intro page). This intro copy helps strengthen the payoff and provides an important context for the reader. If the reader goes no further than page one, he or she should still take away a key message.

Moving beyond the intro page, you can use the word ***"Opportunity"*** (or whatever your key word happens to be) in each spread headline. This is generally the case with the word approach. The word on the cover becomes the pivotal word in a series of headlines. In this case:

- ***The opportunity to innovate***
- ***The opportunity to grow***
- ***The opportunity to connect***
- ***The opportunity to partner***

## Working With Adverbs and Adjectives

Don't think only nouns can go on the front cover. Adverbs and adjectives do quite well there, also. As do some verbs.

You can use words singly or in a phrase. If your key message is about sustained growth, the word "always" might make a good choice for the cover. For example, you can place the adverb ***Always*** on the cover and follow it up with adverbial phrases on the interior pages.

- ***Always growing***
- ***Always innovating***
- ***Always building***
- ***Always moving***
- ***Always helping***
- ***Always whatever***

## Raising an Eyebrow

For variation, you can also use the Always phrases as "eyebrows." An eyebrow is a word or short phrase that sets up a longer headline. It's called an eyebrow because it's normally placed above the headline at the top left of the page or spread.

The eyebrow points your reader's attention in the direction you want it go. It is a general statement, whereas the headline that follows it focuses on something more specific, such as the company's performance, a notable event or a significant accomplishment. Here's a simple example:

**Eyebrow:**
*Always innovating*

**Headline:**
*We're building a better approach to productivity*

# **Approach 3:** Organizing the Annual Report Around People

A popular annual report approach is to organize your book around people—employees, customers or a mix of both. As a concept, **People** can bring your narrative to life and humanize your company. Focusing on people adds more dimension to your story. It provides readers with a better understanding of your company's culture.

That said; try not to use people gratuitously. Your key message still comes first. The people in your narrative should serve a strategic purpose. They should not only support the key message; they should help deliver it.

In any event, avoid the following conversation:

*You::* "It's annual report time again."
*Your company:* "Let's do it about our people this year."

The latter response begs the question, "Why?" Unless your employees serve some strategic purpose, leave them out. Let's say your company acquired another company but the resulting integration proved difficult and somewhat demoralizing. That's a story you could tell using people.

There are many ways to incorporate people into your annual report. Here are some common approaches you can take. I've barely scratched the surface. Again, these ideas are presented to stimulate your own creative thinking.

**TIP:** Should you develop a people concept, it's best to have it begin on the front cover.

### People Example 1: *Meeting Customer Needs*

This approach centers on your customers, and as often as not, on their customers, too. The story can include narrative, case studies, customer testimonials, customer anecdotes, and stories from end users.

The idea here is to highlight the attributes that drive your company's performance. The list can include the usual suspects—innovation, responsiveness, technology, world-class solutions, quality, customer service, experience, etc.—presented from the customer's point of view.

Suppose you are a pharmaceutical company and your key message is to enlighten readers about the many positive ways you serve humankind. Your concept is the phrase "Touching People's Lives." In this scenario, your story should begin, not with your company, but with patients and their families and the impact your medicines has on their lives. You can then link that back to R&D, clinical trials, etc.

### People Example 2: *A Day in the Life*

This scenario chronicles your company's activities and events against an imaginary 24-hour backdrop. This is an excellent way to add a sense of speed, drama or intrigue to the narrative. It's also very useful for showing your company and its people in action.

Say you're writing an annual report for a power company. You would start by making a list of key events and activities that support your key message, and then plug them into your 24-hour time window. Don't restrict your ideas by being too literal with the time. The point is to paint a more comprehensive picture of your company and its people.

For instance, in our power company scenario, we might include things like installing new service for a family's first house, fixing power lines downed by a falling tree in a thunderstorm, helping an elderly customer understand her bill, etc.

To get more mileage from this concept, you should include some type of format device or label, such as a bold header or eyebrow, which provides the day, time, place, and a brief description for each spread. Using a device like this adds authenticity and consistency to your content. For that reason, the format you choose for the device should be consistent throughout the book.

Here's a simple formatting option:

**Tuesday, 2:40 a.m.**
**Pangborn Drive—Dallas, Texas**
**Power crews work through the night to restore power after a heavy storm**

**People Example 3:** *The Face of (Company)*

The **Face** concept focuses on the people behind the company. Simply put, the face of a company is the sum of the many faces that work there. This approach lends itself well to organizing your annual report around operating divisions or segments—or around key attributes or accomplishments. It emphasizes the points that a company's strength is in its people, and that its people control its destiny.

Don't limit yourself to just "The face of (Company)." Other ways of introducing that concept could include:

- *The engine of our future*
- *The builders of our future*
- *Meet team (Company)*
- *A revealing look at (Company)*
- *(Company) Close-up*

# **Approach 4:** Shifting Point of View (POV)

You can use this approach to change readers' perception or understanding of your company. Or to enlighten the reader about specific aspects of your company. Or to provide a glimpse beneath the hood.

The construction is usually in two parts: 1) What readers think or see now, and 2) What you want them to think or see. Here are some sample headline treatments:

### *POV Example 1:* A Development Company

- *You see a stand of pine.*
- *We see where people will live, work and play.*

### *POV Example2:* A Biotechnology Company

- *You see a cornfield.*
- *We see the enzyme that helps keep it healthy.*

### **POV Example 3**: A Global Telecommunications Company

A variation of the "You see/We see" approach is to turn it into a negative statement. The construction is "This is not (something). It's (something else)."

- *This is not a phone line.*
- *It's the entrance to a world of possibilities.*

### **POV Example 4:** A Regional Real Estate Development Company

- *Do you see the sold sign?*
- *We don't. (We see the beginnings of a lasting relationship.)*

## **Approach 5:** Chapters

This stylistic approach provides a good format for telling your company's story. It's ideal for presenting the "big picture."

Just organize the narrative around separate chapters, each with its own number and heading. If one reads nothing more than the Table of Contents, he or she should get a sense of what your key message is.

Use the front cover for your title of your narrative. i.e., **Acme Stove: A Year in Review; Acme Stove: A Growth Story; The Acme Stove Story; Acme Stove: Gaining Momentum, etc.**

Keep in mind, the title needs to provide a natural segue to the chapter headings. In the Acme Stove example, chapter titles might read:

**Chapter 1: A strong performance** (financial performance)
**Chapter 2: Expanding our reach** (marketing initiatives)
**Chapter 3: Innovation in action** (new products)
**Chapter 4: Keeping the future in sight** (vision)

## Approach 6: Shift the story to the front cover.

Why wait for the first text page to start writing? You can begin your story on the front cover with a statement or a block of narrative text. You can also place a quotation on the front cover. Plus you can also put an image on the cover without a headline or text—anything to garner the reader's attention and interest.

For example, the following text marks the 25th anniversary of a successful global bankcard processor, originally spun off by a large national bank. The cover copy captures the dawn of that pivotal event.

**On a chilly January morning in 1979, the card-processing department of North Carolina's First National Bank packed up their desks and moved ten blocks away to a vacant textile mill building.**

**They never looked back.**

## Approach 7: By the Numbers

People like to count, which gives you the opportunity to organize your concept and content into neat little bundles. Here are three examples (numbers are arbitrary):

### A. (Four) Defining Moments

Select the four (or more) watershed events that mark your company's growth and better position it for the future.

Example:

**Defining moment 3: The acquisition of Acme Taffy Company in 2005 nearly doubled our size.**

**B.    Five Fundamental Ideas That Drive Our Company**

Develop five ideas that act as a foundation for your company's growth and organize your content around them. The ideas might already exist. Or you can derive them from your company's vision statement, operating principles, mission statement, etc.

Example:

**Idea 2—Quality is the watchword of growth.**

**Our Company in 10 Words**

Choose 10 qualities that support your concept and define your company. Organize your content around them.

*1)  Innovation*
*1)  Vision*
*2)  Focus*
*3)  Etc.*

## Approach 8: Call-and-Response Phrasing

In music, call and response is a style of singing, wherein one person sings a phrase and another person or a chorus sings a response to that phrase. In the context of your annual report, call and response offers an alternative structure for your top-line messaging.

Think of call and response as a modified type of reveal. The big difference is that in this case, the setup and reveal are on the same page or spread. Because the element of surprise is somewhat diminished, the lines must be able to carry their own weight.

Think of the two lines as the setup and spike in volleyball. Here are some examples:

**E-commerce is moving beyond its EDI foundation.**
**Acme software is already there.**

**E-commerce is growing faster than enterprise resources.**
**Acme Software is filling in the gaps.**

**The world's farmers seek greater efficiency.**
**Acme Tractor delivers.**

## Approach 9: Use Quotations

Quotations are an excellent device for setting credibility, tone and point of view. They can do in a few words what might take you fifty or more. They can be used on the cover, the intro page as well as on each spread. Try to avoid using quotations from obscure people.

**Sample quotation 1:**

**"It is not the strongest of the species that survive, nor the most intelligent, but the one most responsive to change."**

*Charles Darwin*
*Naturalist*

This could be used to launch a discussion of the constructive ways (Company) is dealing with change.

***Sample quotation 2:***

***"Opportunities multiply as they are seized."***

*Sun Tzu*
*"The Art of War"*

This could be used to underscore how *(Company) leverages* its market opportunities.

## Approach 10: Review What Others Have Done

They say good artists borrow; great artists steal. If you're still looking for inspiration, look through your annual report library again. It just may spark an idea.

## Approach 11: Take a Shower

It's true—ask any writer, designer or creative thinker. Some of your best ideas will come to you while you're in the shower. Somewhere out there on the Internet, you can even order a waterproof pen and pad to jot down your ideas before they are washed away.

*Chapter Eight*

# Presenting Your Concepts

Presenting your concepts to your company's annual report committee involves more than just slapping your work down on the table and asking if anyone likes it. Go back to the creative brief you developed and use some of that content to preface your presentation. It's important that the committee members see how well your creative concepts link up to the key message. They also need insight into how your creative thinking evolved. There are several presentation options.

# *Approach 1: Only Present Written Concepts*

Provide written descriptions of your three concepts. Each concept description should fit on a single sheet of paper. The format is very loose. In fact, I've seen hundreds of written concepts and no two were ever alike.

Generally, a written concept includes the concept name (different from the cover headline), a creative rationale for the concept, how the concept works, a description of the cover, the cover headline, one or more spread headlines and anything else you feel will get the concept across.

The advantage of written concepts is that they focus on the idea rather than its execution. This keeps the presentation from bogging down in too many details. Written concepts also help you and your designer avoid unnecessary work. In the best of all possible worlds, the committee will select one of the three written concepts for you to develop further.

**Note:** very literal-minded people have a difficult time understanding a written concept. So be sure of your audience beforehand.

### *What goes in a Written Concept?*

Here's an example for a company that manufactures "invisible" orthodontic devices:

*Concept Name:*
**Beyond Clear**

### Creative Rationale:

"Beyond clear" is our way of stating that (Company) is moving beyond the success of Vista—the world's first invisible (clear) orthodontic device. (Company) is building on its product leadership position, introducing new products like Vista 2, a clear, low-cost alternative that helps dentists in general practice. In addition, the Company has upgraded its software, strengthened its customer support function and forged strong relationships with top dental schools—all while outpacing and outperforming new competitors. Where is the Company headed now? The answer will soon be clear.

*Front cover:*
**Beyond Clear**

*Headlines*

*Pages 2–3:*

**Our quality is unmistakable.**
**So is our leading industry position.**

The Shareholder Letter makes a strong statement that (Company) is positioned for growth and that (Company's) management team is ready to take on any and all competitors.

*Pages 4–5:*

**Our products set the pace for innovation.**
**That's how we stay ahead.**

This spread underscores (Company's) competitive strategy to be the product leader in its industry. It also shows how new products development is helping the company penetrate deeper into doctors' practices.

*Pages 6–7:*

**Our customers have unique needs.**
**So we offer unique solutions.**

This is a mass customization story. (Company) is tailoring products and services to the needs of its unique customer base. The goal: help grow their practices.

*Pages 8–9:*

**Our future is about steady improvement.**
**Our path is beyond clear.**

This spread explains how the Company's strong value proposition, which includes top clinical support, a sound organizational structure, streamlined processes, planning and implementation tools, and faster response times, is the growth driver for the Company's future.

## *Approach 2: Only Present Design Layouts*

In this case, you present your three concepts in layout form, normally a cover, first text page and one sample spread for each concept—all full sized. Like Approach 1, you'll need to write a cover headline and spread headlines. You'll also need to write subheads and intro copy for each concept you'll present; the rest of the text can be "Greek" (unintelligible type). Your designer will create the layouts, incorporating what you write. Together, the front cover, intro copy and sample spread should give the viewer a good sense of how the book will work.

## *Approach 3: Present Both*

I have been in meetings where written concepts were presented first, followed by design layouts. Oftentimes, this is the best approach, as it connects all the dots in the minds of your audience.

*Chapter Nine*

# **Annual Report Gallery**

Most of the annual report examples employed in this book were fabricated to support a particular point or idea. Now it's time to explore—and learn from—some real-world examples. The annual report examples that follow were selected because they contain good illustrations of some of the concepts and approaches discussed in this book. But as with everything else in the real world, don't look for a seamless match with the theoretical.

# Example 1–Neenah Paper 2007 Annual Report

### *All Together. Now.*

Neenah provides an excellent example of how to extend a cover concept through your narrative spreads. A bold copy introduction pays off the cover phrase: ***All together. Now.*** Here's a portion of the intro: "…We continue to gather the elements needed to support our long-range vision—from people and new products and technology to new channels and geographic areas. We are bringing them together. Now. They are essential building blocks for a bright future." The spread headlines that follow also support the key message and adhere to the cover construction, e.g., ***Connecting the dots. Profitably. Looking at the big picture. Up close. Adding capability. Everywhere.***

Example 1.1: Neenah Paper front cover
Design: Addison, NYC

in the three short
years since
our founding, neenah
paper has
changed greatly.

/ 2

We've grown, to be sure, with important acquisitions in fine paper and technical products. And our portfolio of businesses has become more balanced and profitable. Most importantly, we continue to gather the elements needed to support our long-range vision – from people to new products and technology to new channels and geographic areas. We are bringing them all together. Now. They are essential building blocks for a bright future.

/ 3

Example 1.2: Neenah Paper intro spread

/ 12

Looking at the big picture. up close.

We're building a global company, one product line at a time. At Neenah Paper, we continue to direct our company into strong niche markets, like filtration, graphics & identification products, wall covering and premium printing and writing papers. Rather than manage our businesses geographically, we've organized our global businesses along product lines. Technical Products, for example, now breaks down into five categories—filtration, component materials, tape, graphics & identification, and wall covering—regardless of where the products are manufactured or sold. This arrangement gives us more flexibility in sourcing and sales, and more balance for managing profitable growth opportunities. Today, we don't make decisions based on what's best for a particular country or region. We look at what's best for Neenah as a whole.

/ 13

Example 1.3: Neenah Paper narrative spread

## Example 2–Sara Lee Corporation 2007 Summary Annual Report

### *something's COOKING*

Sara Lee offers a great example of how to entice annual report readers to look beyond the cover. The headline on the front cover — *something's COOKING* —piques readers' curiosity and leads to two reveals on the inside: *something's BREWING and something's IN THE AIR.* The former highlights Sara Lee's fast-growing, single-serve Sensco coffee brand. The latter focuses on their new Ambi Pur air freshener brand. Together, the three headlines also work metaphorically. Their message: a new Sara Lee is taking shape.

Example 2.1: Sara Lee front cover
Design: Coates & Coates

something's
# IN THE AIR

New Ambi Pur Puresse
is a range of air fresheners
specially formulated to reduce
the risk of skin allergies. This
innovative, consumer insight-
driven product from Sara Lee's
international air care brand
will be rolled out around the
world in fiscal 2008.

something's
**BREWING**

PHILIPS
Senseo

DOUWE
EGBERTS
Sen
FINEST COFFEE

Mountain Roast
SUMATRA BLEND
Net Wt. 3.92 oz (111g)

Senseo – the convenient
single-serve coffee innovation
from Sara Lee and Philips
Electronics – offers con-
sumers around the world a
wide variety of frothy gourmet
coffees, made quick and
easy with the Senseo coffee
machine. Senseo coffee sales
increased 27% to $445 million
in fiscal 2007.

Example 2.2: Sara Lee intro spread

# BRINGING MORE TO THE (BREAKFAST) TABLE

The *Jimmy Dean* brand is a great example of how Sara Lee is rejuvenating its top brands and redefining its core categories. The brand has dramatically broadened its scope, evolving from a breakfast sausage into a breakfast platform. Offering time-constrained consumers convenient, quick-to-serve, hot and hearty breakfast solutions, *Jimmy Dean's* breakfast products now include Breakfast Bowls, Skillets, Omelets and various Breakfast Sandwiches, including the new "better-for-you" *Jimmy Dean* D-lights.

4   Sara Lee Corporation

Example 2.3: Sara Lee narrative spread

# Example 3—Quaker Chemical Corporation 2006 Annual Report

## Keeping good company

You don't have to look very far for the payoff to this smart cover line. It, too, is on the cover. It reads, **Keeping good company. It's how Quaker expands opportunities—with proven presence, shared insight, and unrelenting focus.** Bold copy on the intro page sets up the key message: *"*At Quaker, our go-anywhere, do-any-thing, knowledge-driven, burn-the-midnight-oil culture is turning heads. And profits." The headlines for the narrative spreads link back to the key message, i.e., **Keeping good company. With proven presence. It's the power Quaker has built in every corner of the world.** (Note the effective use of sentence fragments.)

Keeping good company

It's how Quaker expands opportunities—
with proven presence, shared insight, and unrelenting focus.

Quaker Chemical Corporation 2006 Annual Report

Example 3.1: Quaker Chemical front cover
Design and production: Rector Communications Inc.

Our Destination

A single worldwide company that delivers everywhere the best from anywhere, that creates value in every process we serve, and that every customer will find indispensable. We will be the undisputed leader in the businesses we choose and will be known widely for our growth and financial success and as a premier place to work.

At Quaker, our go-anywhere, do-anything, knowledge-driven, burn-the-midnight-oil culture is turning heads. And profits.

Example 3.2: Quaker Chemical intro page

## Keeping good company. With shared insight.
It's a source of innovation in our technologies and markets.

At Quaker, we collaborate continually with customers, equipment manufacturers, raw material suppliers—even service and support providers. Those relationships build insight. Insight builds innovation. And, innovation brings the technological advances that help us and our customers win in the marketplace.

Here's an example from the steel business that illustrates the point well. A major European manufacturer of hot rolling equipment had been wrestling with quality issues on new, thinner gauge steels. We joined them to develop new lubricants and innovative application equipment that significantly improved surface quality. The improvement was so substantial that more than a dozen continuous strip mills in Europe, Asia, and South America adopted the technology. And, 45 additional conventional mills have since been converted to use the process. Now, the mills adopting this technology have become proving grounds for further refinement in equipment and lubrication.

Collaboration can even take us out of one industry and into another—quickly and efficiently. When our coatings group developed a new, fast-curing UV coating for pipes, they realized that similar technology could be used to maintain plant floors—greatly reducing resurfacing downtime. Although Quaker had no experience in floor coatings, we keep company with plenty of customers who do. A closely aligned customer was excited about the prospects and worked with us—allowing the idea to move quickly into development and onward to a successful product trial.

We cast a wide net in search of technical knowledge. But, perhaps, no other single source of technological innovation is as fruitful as our relationships with customers. They have the drive, the need, and the energy to make every process and end product better. Chemical Management Services (CMS) is a case in point. CMS contracts put Quaker in charge of virtually all chemicals used in a customer's operation, whether a single production line or an entire plant. We may not supply all the chemicals being managed, but we do own the results of our management efforts. In fact, at our CMS sites we are typically paid according to the value—in savings and improvements, we produce.

Our long history of working closely with the world's leading mill equipment manufacturers has broadened our knowledge and led us to countless innovations. One 20-year relationship has helped Quaker establish a leadership position in steel rolling mills worldwide.

We're happy with such arrangements because we are successful at producing results. In one recent case, we were able to identify savings of over $500,000 per year—for one U.S. automaker at just one of its plants. Annual savings of a similar magnitude are likely to be realized at similar plants operated by this customer and by other automakers across the globe.

That case is typical. Of the 31 of our CMS contracts we have that were up for renewal at North American locations last year, every one was renewed for three years. Quaker innovation improves the customer's bottom line—and that helped win contract renewals.

For more information, go to www.quakerchem.com  < 9 >

"The most exciting ideas come from collaborating with customers and equipment suppliers. As we each bring in what we know best, we create things that are new, valuable, and mutually beneficial."

Example 3.3: Quaker Chemical narrative spread

# Example 4–Bank of America 2007 Annual Report

## *Insights + Innovations = Opportunities*

Bank of America's 2007 annual report is a fine example of a cohesive concept. It centers on their associates, who, collectively, are an important source of insights and innovations. Thumbnail pictures of associates fill the front and back covers. The cover line reads, Insights + Innovations = Opportunities. The intro copy reads, "We are a company of more than 200,000 associates, serving a vibrant community of customers and clients around the world. Our size and scope—unmatched by any other bank—give us insights that help us innovate and create opportunities for all." The cover is die-cut in the shape of the Bank of America logo, which shows through from the intro page. Along with narrative text, each spread contains a prominent sidebar that presents a concise case study structured around Insights, Innovations and Opportunities—further paying off the cover.

Insights + Innovations ⇌ Opportunities

2007 Annual Report

**Bank of America**
Bank of Opportunity™

Example 4.1: Bank of America front cover
Design and production: Story Worldwide

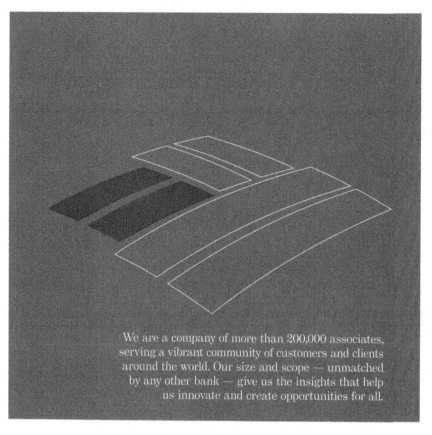

We are a company of more than 200,000 associates, serving a vibrant community of customers and clients around the world. Our size and scope — unmatched by any other bank — give us the insights that help us innovate and create opportunities for all.

Insights + Innovations ⇌ Opportunities

**Bank of America**
Bank of Opportunity™

Example 4.2: Bank of America intro page

Insights + Innovations ⇌ Opportunities

## Insights

- Our customers say they like the ease of accessing Bank of America anytime, anywhere.
- Customers using a mobile platform want the same security they enjoy using Online Banking at home.

## Innovations

- Bank of America created a pocket-size mobile bank that translates to any screen.
- An end-to-end secure connection and the $0 Liability Online Banking Guarantee protect customers from promptly reported unauthorized activity.
- Mobile Banking customers can also send money to their Online Banking payees and transferees.

## Opportunities

- More than 240 million cell phones are in use in the United States; our mobile services can reach 75 percent of them.
- Mobile Banking services work around the world for users with an international calling plan.
- By anticipating our customers' needs and demands, we can grow in a rapidly changing

# BANKING AS MOBILE AS YOU ARE

## STAYING IN TOUCH WITH YOUR FINANCES WHEN YOU'RE ON THE ROAD NEEDN'T BE AN OLYMPIAN TASK.

**Banking on the Go**

Bank of America active Mobile Banking users, 2007 *(in thousands)*

| | |
|---|---|
| December | 617 |
| October | 487 |
| August | 388 |
| June | 172 |

Source: Bank of America

Next August, when many of his compatriots are thinking sun and surf, Brett Heyl plans to be paddling for gold. A member of the 2004 U.S. Olympic kayak team that competed in Athens, he now has his sights set on Beijing for the 2008 Olympic Games. And as one of 12 Bank of America Hometown Hopefuls™ supported by the bank's sponsorship of the U.S. Olympic Team, he'll have the chance to bring his family and friends to China. "Staying connected is an important part of my training," said Heyl, 26. "I'm always at my best when I'm surrounded by my support team."

Heyl, whose hometown is Norwich, Vermont, has found other ways to stay connected when he's on the road for competitions and training. An avid user of Bank of America Online and Mobile Banking, Heyl uses his laptop and iPhone™ to access accounts, pay bills, transfer money and locate ATMs and banking centers across the nation.

With Mobile Banking, protecting customer data is paramount. Bank of America's end-to-end security ensures that information stays encrypted as it travels between cell phone and bank. Customers can also set up the service to send them e-mail or text message alerts related to their accounts. Heyl receives an e-mail whenever a direct deposit is credited to one of his accounts. He also gets a reminder if a bill is due or his deposit balance drops below a predetermined amount.

It's a great service for someone who's on the go every day. "I can be training in Charlotte one day, home in New England the next and traveling to a competition across the globe a week later," said Heyl, who's been a kayaker since he was 9. "Bank of America's Online and Mobile Banking services go everywhere I do and allow me to check my finances anytime it's convenient for me."

That's precisely why only six months after launching the service, Bank of America had more than 600,000 active Mobile Banking users — more than all other U.S. banks combined. Add them to 24 million Online Banking customers (almost 40 percent of total U.S. online banking users), and it's easy to see that Bank of America is where customers want and need it to be.

◁ Olympic kayaker Brett Heyl can stay in touch with his finances even when he's training at the U.S. National Whitewater Center near Charlotte, North Carolina.

## Taking the bank to the customer

Bank of America was the first bank to offer Mobile Banking service to its millions of online customers through the widest variety of carriers and devices — more than 460 types of phones, including the Apple iPhone™. "We're taking convenience and control to a new level by letting customers stay connected with their finances even when they're on the go," said e-Commerce/ATM executive Lance Drummond.

Like Bank of America's Online Banking — recently voted the best consumer Internet bank site in the world by *Global Finance* magazine for the second year in a row — Mobile Banking is protected by the award-winning SiteKey® security service and the $0 Liability Online Banking Guarantee, which covers any unauthorized activity originating from Online Banking, including bill payment, when reported within 60 days of the statement date. For more peace of mind, Bank of America created SafePass℠, a security system that sends a one-time passcode to a cell phone or integrated debit card when customers need to make large transfers or other sensitive transactions.

Mobile Banking is not available with accounts located in Washington or Idaho.

Bank of America 2007  21

Example 4.3: Bank of America narrative spread

# Example 5–Kraft Foods 2006 Annual Report

### *Meet our new boss:*

This annual report delivers Kraft's key message in a fun yet effective way. The compelling cover line sets up a perfect reveal. Open the annual report and you'll learn that the ultimate boss at Kraft is the consumer. The intro copy reads,

> *"She's a 64-pound soccer star. A garage band singer in Friedrichshafen. A Tulsa mother of three. Our boss comes in every possible variety. She's unique; he is an individual. And while their faces are familiar, their world is changing fast. What will quench tomorrow's thirst? Satisfy tomorrow's hunger? There's only one way to know, and that's to see the world through their eyes."*

The highly visual spreads combined with sparse bold narrative copy support Kraft's consumer-centric point of view without overwhelming the reader. The takeaway from this annual report is clear: Kraft grows by identifying, understanding and fulfilling consumers' needs.

Example 5.1: Kraft front cover
Concept and Design: Genesis Inc.

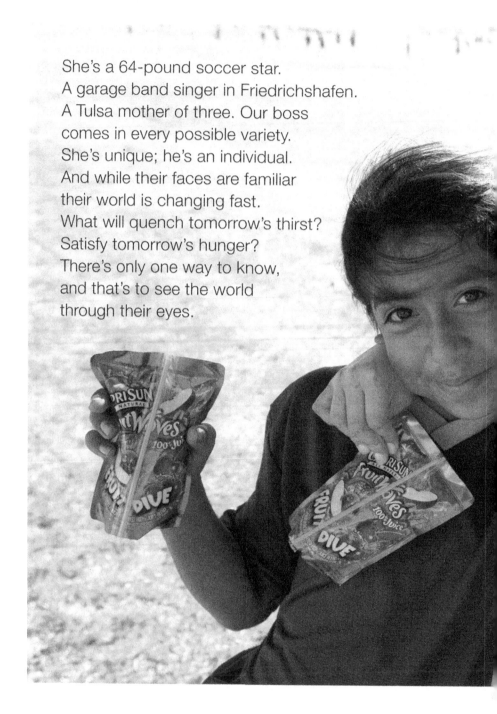

She's a 64-pound soccer star.
A garage band singer in Friedrichshafen.
A Tulsa mother of three. Our boss
comes in every possible variety.
She's unique; he's an individual.
And while their faces are familiar
their world is changing fast.
What will quench tomorrow's thirst?
Satisfy tomorrow's hunger?
There's only one way to know,
and that's to see the world
through their eyes.

Example 5.2: Kraft intro spread

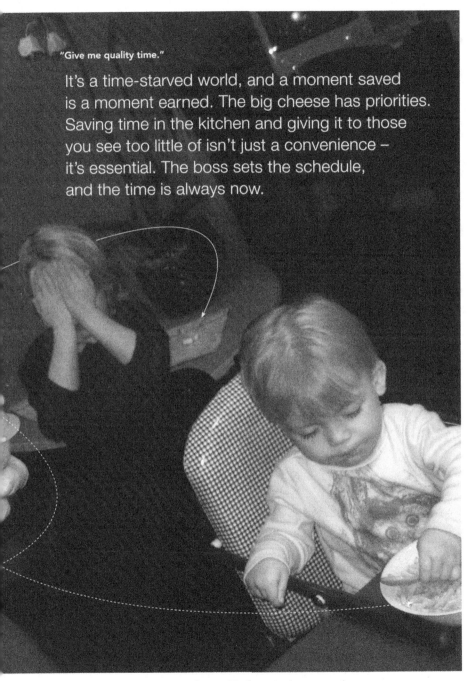

"Give me quality time."

It's a time-starved world, and a moment saved is a moment earned. The big cheese has priorities. Saving time in the kitchen and giving it to those you see too little of isn't just a convenience – it's essential. The boss sets the schedule, and the time is always now.

Example 5.3: Kraft narrative spread

## Example 6—CVS Caremark Corp. 2007 Annual Report

### *The power of one*

In 2007, CVS merged with Caremark to become the largest integrated provider of prescriptions and related health services in the United States. This fact is the foundation for the cover line, ***The power of one***. The "one" concept continues inside where bold subheads indicate that CVS/Caremark is number one in many things. They are #1 ***in the number of prescriptions filled, #1 in retail clinics, #1 in specialty pharmacy, #1 in store count, and #1 in retail loyalty***. CVS/Caremark extends the one concept even further, with bold page headlines that read ***One company, One view of the patient***, and for the start of the shareholder letter, ***One goal***. This is an extremely good example of how to weave a cover concept through the entire annual report—including the shareholder letter. By scanning just the headlines and subheads, you'll still come away with a good sense of CVS/Caremark's key message.

The Power of One

CVS Caremark Corporation 2007 Annual Report

Example 6.1: CVS Caremark front cover
Concept and Design: see see eye / Atlanta, GA

# Unmatched Breadth of Capabilities

With the 2007 merger of CVS Corporation and Caremark Rx, Inc., we've become an integrated provider of prescriptions and related health services with an unmatched breadth of capabilities. We're the market leader in multiple categories and able to provide payors and patients with solutions that no pharmacy retailer or pharmacy benefits manager on its own could offer. It's "The Power of One."

The combination will enable us to provide end-to-end solutions that impact everything from pharmacy plan design to the ultimate delivery of products and services to customers. Our capabilities include industry-leading clinical and health management programs, specialty pharmacy expertise, leadership in retail clinics, customer service excellence, and our deep knowledge of the consumer gained through the more than four million customers who visit our stores every day.

We invite you to turn the page to learn more about our new company and our plans for improving the delivery of pharmacy and health care services in the United States.

# #1 in Prescriptions

CVS Caremark fills or manages more than 1 billion prescriptions annually through our retail and specialty pharmacy stores, mail order facilities, and PBM retail network pharmacies. That figure makes us the undisputed leader in our industry. U.S. pharmacy sales are expected to grow at approximately 5 percent annually for the foreseeable future, and we are well positioned to benefit from this favorable trend. We expect to gain share in our retail and PBM businesses through our combined company's unique offerings, which competitors cannot currently replicate.

Example 6.2: CVS Caremark intro page

# <sup>#</sup>1 in Retail Clinics

MinuteClinic, the nation's leading chain of retail-based health clinics, operated 462 locations in 25 states at year-end. Nearly all are located right inside our stores, making it "CVS easy" to seek treatment for common illnesses or to receive routine vaccinations. Open seven days a week, MinuteClinic requires no appointment. Its clinicians – primarily nurse practitioners – have handled more than 1.5 million patient visits to date and over 500,000 in the final four months of 2007 alone. With our broader health care focus, many more MinuteClinics are on the way in 2008 with an expanded list of services.

# <sup>#</sup>1 in Specialty Pharmacy

CVS Caremark leads the industry with approximately $8 billion in specialty pharmacy sales through our 20 specialty mail order pharmacies, our 56 specialty pharmacy stores, and CVS/pharmacy locations. Specialty costs are rising rapidly for payors, and we're uniquely positioned to help our PBM clients control spending with our advanced utilization management guidelines, clinical expertise, and Accordant® health management programs.

# #1 in Store Count

With nearly 6,300 CVS/pharmacy locations and 56 specialty pharmacy stores from coast to coast, we operate more stores than any other U.S. drugstore chain. More than 60 percent are freestanding, making it "CVS easy" for customers to fill prescriptions, replenish the medicine cabinet, or stop in to consult with one of our beauty advisors. With free time in such short supply these days, 60 percent of our locations offer drive-thru pharmacies and 72 percent provide the convenience of 24-hour or extended-hours drugstores.

# #1 in Retail Loyalty

The most popular loyalty program in retail expanded further in 2007 as ExtraCare card usage exceeded 63 percent of front-end sales. More than 50 million active cardholders are taking advantage of in-store sales while skipping the hassle of clipping coupons. They also receive offerings with their receipts targeted to their specific shopping preferences along with quarterly ExtraBucks. ExtraBucks can be used for virtually any front-end purchase just like cash, and customers tell us they love them!

Example 6.3: CVS Caremark narrative spread

# Example 7—Southern Company 2006 Annual Report:

### *01 every second...*

Southern Company grabs the reader's attention with this intriguing cover line. It serves as both the beginning of the narrative copy and as a setup to the reveal inside. The takeaway here is simply that people's need for energy is steadily growing and Southern Company is working hard to meet that demand—***every second, of every minute, of every hour, of every day.*** The Letter to Shareholders opens with bold text, continuing the time concept: ***"EVERY MOMENT of every day, we strive to be the leader in our industry and to deliver outstanding results for our shareholders and our customers."*** Other spreads drill down to explore Southern Company's business more fully. ***"Every minute,"*** for instance, is about improving energy efficiency for commercial and residential customers.

Example 7.1: Southern Company front cover
Writing & Project Management: Terri Cohilas
Design: Leap Design, Atlanta, GA

of every minute, of ever

CONTENTS

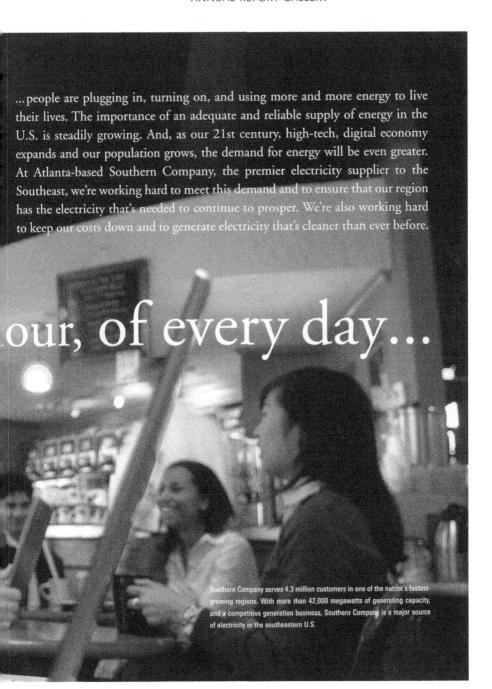

...people are plugging in, turning on, and using more and more energy to live their lives. The importance of an adequate and reliable supply of energy in the U.S. is steadily growing. And, as our 21st century, high-tech, digital economy expands and our population grows, the demand for energy will be even greater. At Atlanta-based Southern Company, the premier electricity supplier to the Southeast, we're working hard to meet this demand and to ensure that our region has the electricity that's needed to continue to prosper. We're also working hard to keep our costs down and to generate electricity that's cleaner than ever before.

our, of every day...

Southern Company serves 4.3 million customers in one of the nation's fastest-growing regions. With more than 42,000 megawatts of generating capacity, and a competitive generation business, Southern Company is a major source of electricity in the southeastern U.S.

Example 7.2: Southern Company intro spread

MEETING DEMAND THROUGH EFFICIENCY

At Southern Company, we believe it is our business to always consider the future and plan appropriately. Forecasts tell us that the population of the Southeast is continuing on a growth course. We're taking steps now to ensure that we grow along with the region. Our 42,000 megawatts of capacity are serving us well right now, and we're making plans for additional capacity to meet future demand. We're also growing something else at Southern Company. We're growing our efforts to educate customers to become more efficient with their energy use. We're working with builders a developers to ensure that new homes and office buildings warehouses are more energy-efficient than they've ever been. W helping our commercial and industrial customers find efficien by calculating when they can reduce usage without sacrificing p ductivity. And, for our residential customers, we're finding me and better ways to keep their electricity costs as low as possi All the way down to the light bulb.

00:01:00

# every minute

Americans' energy efficiency efforts save more than $57,000 on utility bills and enough energy to avoid greenhouse gas emissions equivalent to those from 43 cars.

Thanks in part to ENERGY STAR®, a joint program of the U.S. Environmental Protection Agency and the U.S. Department of Energy, we are saving money and protecting the environment through energy-efficient products and practices.

THIS LITTLE LIGHT

across the Southern Company system, we're asking customers take the pledge." We're telling our customers that changing one incandescent bulb to an ENERGY STAR-qualified compact fluorescent light bulb can save as much as $30 on energy costs the life of the bulb. In fact, switching to an ENERGY STAR-qualified bulb in the five most used fixtures in a home make a real impact. If every American household made that ch, we'd save about $6.5 billion each year in energy costs and prevent greenhouse gas emissions equivalent to the emissions of 8 million cars.

Southern Company subsidiary Georgia Power is a leading driver of "Change a Light" pledges nationwide. The ENERGY STAR "Change a Light" program is a nationwide campaign to build awareness about energy efficiency and to educate consumers on ways to save electricity and lower their energy costs.

Every light changed is a step in the right direction.

Example 7.3: Southern Company narrative spread

## Example 8—Goodrich Corporation 2005 Annual Report

*UP*

Never has such a small word conveyed so much as the **UP** on the front cover of the 2005 Goodrich annual report. As a concept, **UP** seamlessly integrates with the narrative copy. It becomes a platform that supports a variety of messages. It speaks to Goodrich's leading position in the aerospace industry. It underlies their strong financial performance and growing margins. And it portends a bright outlook for the future. Used like a bold rubber stamp, **UP** appears at the top of nearly every page of the narrative copy. This is another good example of how to weave a cover concept through the entire annual report. Quickly scan the narrative pages, and you'll know in an instant what Goodrich's year was like. Even better, you'll learn where the company is going—**UP.**

# UP

Goodrich Corporation Annual Report 2005

Example 8.1: Goodrich front cover
Design: see see eye / Atlanta, GA

# UP

[ SALES ]

Goodrich sales continued to climb in 2005. Sales rose 15% to $5.4 billion for the year, marking our third consecutive year of increased sales and surpassing the $5 billion milestone as a company focused on aerospace. Strong growth in our markets continued to drive our forward momentum.

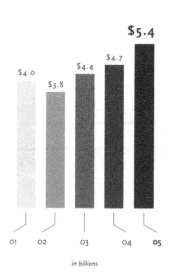

$5.4

$4.7

$4.0

$3.8

$4.4

01  02  03  04  05

*in billions*

Additional contract wins enhanced our positions on exciting
new introductions, including the Boeing 787 Dreamliner and
the Airbus A350. Several Goodrich products took to the skies
for the first time aboard the Airbus A380. An extensive array
of Goodrich systems and components will not only help them
fly and keep them safe, but should also have a significant role
in our expected revenue growth in the years ahead.

# UP

[ POSITIONS ]

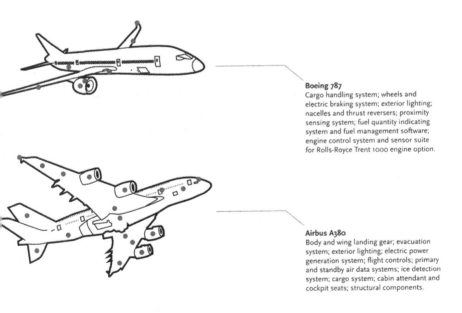

**Boeing 787**
Cargo handling system; wheels and
electric braking system; exterior lighting;
nacelles and thrust reversers; proximity
sensing system; fuel quantity indicating
system and fuel management software;
engine control system and sensor suite
for Rolls-Royce Trent 1000 engine option.

**Airbus A380**
Body and wing landing gear; evacuation
system; exterior lighting; electric power
generation system; flight controls; primary
and standby air data systems; ice detection
system; cargo system; cabin attendant and
cockpit seats; structural components.

Goodrich Corporation          1

Example 8.2: Goodrich intro spread

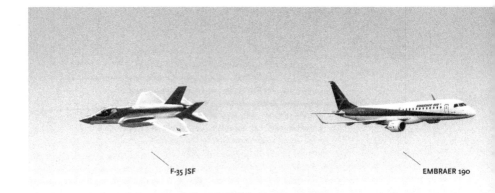

F-35 JSF                    EMBRAER 190

# UP

[ MARKETS ]

With one of the most strategically diversified product portfolios in the industry, Goodrich is well-positioned to capture market share. Our strategy for balanced growth focuses on expansion in all three of our major market channels. We delivered on this strategy in 2005, with commercial aircraft original equipment sales increasing 20%, commercial aircraft aftermarket sales up 16% and military and space sales climbing 8% over 2004.

2    Annual Report 2005

**Homeland Security**

# UP

[ OPPORTUNITIES ]

**Aftermarket**

**Unmanned Vehicles**

**Surveillance/Reconnaissance**

Goodrich has a world of opportunities on the horizon,
ranging from new program awards such as the nacelles
and thrust reversers for the GEnx-powered Airbus A350
to innovative long-term support agreements with global
airline customers and exciting new product applications.
Expansion opportunities also include our Laser Perimeter
Awareness System for homeland security, systems and
components for the latest Unmanned Aerial Vehicles and
innovative imaging technology for intelligence, surveillance
and reconnaissance systems.

Goodrich Corporation        3

Example 8.3: Goodrich narrative spread

# Example 9–Crawford & Company 2006 Annual Report

### *Working Together*

If you use a phrase on the cover, make sure you link the narrative to it in some way. In Crawford's case, the linkup was accomplished by making the cover phrase, ***Working Together***, part of the individual spread headlines. The intro page also pays off the Working Together phrase. "With over 700 offices in 63 countries, our associates work together to find the best solutions for clients...." Clearly, this is a story about people—Crawford's people—and the commitment they make to meeting their clients' needs. The headlines all follow the same construction as the cover, but each presents the benefits of Working Together in a different way, e.g., ***Working Together, Better Than Ever*** and ***Working Together, Offering More.***

Crawford & Company 2006 Annual Report

Example 9.1: Crawford & Co, front cover
Design & Production: see see eye / Atlanta, GA

*Crawford & Company:*

## Working Together

With over 700 offices in 63 countries, our associates work together to find the best solution for clients. Allow us to illustrate how we achieve the best possible outcomes for our clients.

2006 Annual Report  7

Example 9.2: Crawford & Co. intro page

Global Property & Casualty

GLOBAL PROPERTY & CASUALTY

*Total Revenue (in thousands):*

$513,680

*Number of Associates:*

5,286

*Executive General Adjusters (EGA):*

429

*Clients:*

5,195

*Clients in Excess of $1 Million:*

86

*Claims Per Day:*

2,482

*Type of Services:*

Property Claims Management

Catastrophe Management Services

Casualty Claims Management

Auto Appraisals and Inspections

Centralized Claims Administration

"We recognize Crawford's ability to understand
our customers' needs and execute a professional,
timely, and effective claim solution."

DAVID BONEHILL
Chief Claims Manager
Ecclesiastical Insurance Group
Gloucester, U.K.

"We challenged Crawford to meet our unique
handling requirements in the U.K. and U.S.,
and they have delivered by not only promptly
handling our claims, but by offering innovative
and cost-effective solutions with our insured's
best interests in mind."

BOB FOSTER
Group Director of Claims
Brit Insurance
London, U.K.

8  Crawford & Company

# Working Together, Better than Ever

Crawford Global Property & Casualty is the largest independent third-party provider of property and casualty solutions in the world. Operating in 63 countries today with revenues over half a billion dollars, GPC is unique in its ability to provide multinational corporations with turnkey worldwide solutions. Crawford continues to expand its service delivery in European, Asian Pacific, and Latin American markets. Our three global product lines, Corporate Multinational Risks, Global Marine and Transportation, and Global Technical Services, coupled with our field office locations around the world, are set to offer exceptional service on claims of all sizes.

"I have been with Crawford over 33 years and I have seen many changes: One constant is the common desire of all associates to work together to deliver the best service possible to our clients. Accomplishing this goal daily is a great source of satisfaction for all of my staff. They are dedicated to this goal and take personal pride in achieving it."

MARIE CAMPBELL (2005, 2006 Circle of Excellence recipient)
Branch Manager
Kentucky and Southern Indiana
Crawford & Company
Lexington, Kentucky

"As a relatively new employee to Crawford & Company, I see a common thread amongst sales and management of all levels. That thread or common denominator is the desire to create partnerships with our clients, to understand their expectations, and to gain their trust. In return, we offer personalized service as well as a wide array of products and services at high-quality standards that far outweigh the competition. Relationships and trust are what builds long-term business."

HELEN VOUNIOZOS
Assistant Vice President
National Account Executive
Crawford & Company
Phoenix, Arizona

2006 Annual Report   9

Example 9.3: Crawford & Co. narrative spread

# Example 10–CBL & Associates Properties, Inc. 2005 Annual Report

## *That's impressive...Our dominant market strategy*

Sometimes your readers can use a break from the predictable structure of the narrative. Sometimes your message can, as well. That's when it's time to erect a few billboard spreads. These combine a dramatic visual with scant copy. At their best, billboard spreads deliver a singular point to readers. For instance, the billboard spread above concisely explains CBL's dominant market strategy for growth. ***"For CBL, it's not about the size or location of a retail market. It's about our ability to dominate it."***

***that's*** impressive

CBL & Associates Properties, Inc. 2005 Annual Report

For CBL, it's not about the size or location of a retail market. It's about our ability to dominate it. So we choose our development and acquisition sites carefully. We look for growth opportunities – that is, well-defined geographical segments where there is an expanding population of consumers.

3

## *our dominant market strategy*

Example 10.1: CBL & Assoc. billboard spread
Design & Production: see see eye / Atlanta, GA

# Example 11—Neenah Paper 2004 Annual Report

### *Listen to our customers*

This billboard spread also delivers a singular message: Neenah Paper has put in place a strong, responsive customer service program. Or as the spread puts it, ***"When our customers speak, Neenah Paper aims to hear every word."*** In addition to putting emphasis on a particular point, billboard spreads make an annual report more interesting than if it were just straight narrative text. If nothing else, think of them as pleasant rest stops on your annual report journey.

# 4.

[ *listen* to our customers ]

When our customers speak, Neenah Paper
aims to hear every word. This is why we
have structured a strong customer service
program, one that's as critical to meeting
our customers' needs as the innovative
solutions and the quality of the products
we provide.

Neenah Paper, Inc. 2004 Annual Report

Example 11.1: Neenah Paper billboard spread
Design & Production: see see eye / Atlanta, GA

## Chapter Ten

# Giving Your Concept Legs

Once you've established your three concepts, the next step is to extend those concepts throughout the annual report. To do that effectively, you'll need to develop two things:

**1.  A pagination diagram**
**2.  A copy outline**

This chapter will discuss pagination. The next chapter will cover the development of your copy outline.

## Who's on First?

For our purposes, a pagination diagram is a series of small vertical boxes that represent the actual pages of your annual report. It's often referred to as a "road map," as it shows the path your annual report content will take.

Creating a pagination diagram is an essential part of the annual report process. It helps you organize and visualize the content and decide what subjects should be covered on each page. It also helps you share your annual report thinking with other people. Unless you are one of those rare individuals who can keep track of a million things at once in his or her head, you don't want to skip this step.

A typical pagination diagram usually depicts the following elements:

– **Front cover (FC)**
– **Inside front cover (IFC)**
– **Page 1 (intro page)**
– **Pages 2 & 3 (first spread)**
– **Additional spreads**
– **Inside back cover (IBC)**
– **Back cover (BC)**

You can draw the diagram freehand or create simple boxes with the drawing tools of your word processing software. First, draw the front cover, inside front cover and page 1, which is the first text page. Join two boxes down the middle to create a two-page "spread." Do not link the spreads together in tandem; leave some white space between them.

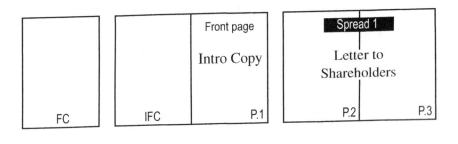

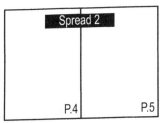

Figure 1: Generic pagination diagram (roadmap)

## A Quick Bindery Lesson

It's time for a bindery lesson. Bindery is a printing term. It refers to how your annual report will be assembled. If your annual report will be "saddle stitched" (stapled down the spine), it will be made up of four-page "signatures." So the total number of pages in your annual report must always be divisible by four. In other words, you just can't add a single page; you have to add another four-page signature.

If your annual report will be "perfect bound" (pages glued together along the spine), you can add one sheet at a time. Keep in mind, however, that one sheet printed front and back yields two pages.

## Creating Your Pagination Diagram

First, make multiple copies of your blank pagination diagram. You'll use them to explore different ways of putting your content together. Think of the pages of your annual report as "real estate." Build your annual report frugally. Don't give every subject the same weight. Or space.

With that in mind, fill in your blank pagination diagram. Label each page or spread with the subject matter you'll discuss there. IMPORTANT: At this point, we're not concerned with style, design, headlines, subheads or copy. We are simply carving up our content to fit in our allotted real estate.

What if there's more content than real estate? You have two options: 1) start cutting and rearranging the content or 2) add more pages.

## Filling in the Blanks

Here's an example of what a filled-in pagination diagram might look like. Let's say we're talking about a metals company that has four reporting or operating segments: 1) rolled steel, 2) flat steel, 3) tube and channel and 4) fabricated metal.

The company is rising out of a two-year slump. Revenues are up, but the company still has plenty of room to grow. Using the simple word-on-the-cover approach, we find the words "***Gaining Momentum***" to be an apt descriptor of where the company is now.

One common way to organize the book would be by operating segments. That's kind of a "Who's buried in Grant's tomb?" approach, as it's the most obvious and expected. If you go that route, make sure it doesn't become a corporate capabilities brochure (unless the company points you in that direction). Corporate capabilities brochures are sales and marketing focused, while annual reports are investor focused.

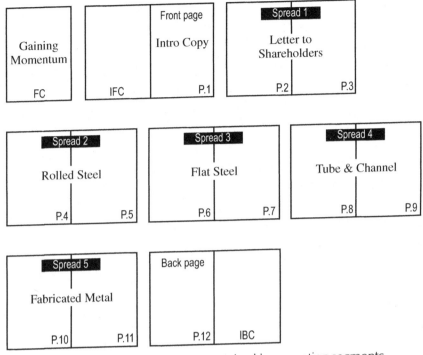

Figure 2: Pagination diagram organized by operating segments

## Telling a more compelling story

Another way to tell this story is to dig down a level and explore what drove the company's momentum across all of its reporting segments. Now you are not just writing about historical performance, but letting the reader in on the bigger picture: the things that make your company successful.

Since we have devoted four spreads to performance, we should identify the four drivers of that performance. In this example, we might end up with these:

1. *Employees*
2. *Innovation*
3. *Quality*
4. *Partnerships*

By organizing the narrative story around these four drivers, you give annual report readers a better context in which to judge the company's performance.

Remember, performance, by itself, is just numbers. Here, we want to give readers the story behind those numbers. By offering readers a new point of view, we make it easier for them to understand the opportunities faced by the company.

The four drivers are just examples. Don't be too quick to adopt my example. Instead, focus on what can contribute to the company's ***"Gaining Momentum"*** concept. You might come up with these same four drivers. Or you might come up with more. If that happens, simply increase the number of spreads. That's easy for me to say, but your company's CFO might have other ideas.

By adding more pages, you are increasing the cost of the annual report. And that's a subject no one is eager to hear about. You'll have an opportunity to present your reasons for expanding the annual report budget. You have about a 50-50 chance of getting an approval.

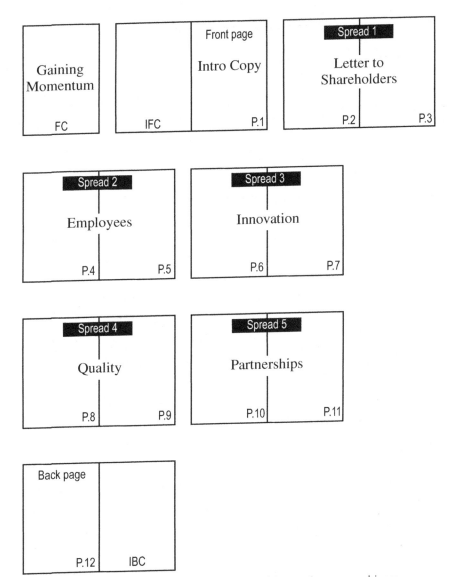

Figure 3: Pagination diagram organized by performance drivers

## Other types of pages within the annual report:

### Letter to Shareholders

As you can see, the Letter to Shareholders is included in the example pagination diagram as a two-page spread. It can just as easily take up two or three spreads. The length of the Letter is up to the CEO (although he or she may not write the first draft).

According to most analysts and shareowners, the Letter is the most important (and most read) communication in the annual report. That said, the position of the Letter within the book varies. It can begin on the intro page (page 1). Or it can appear at the end of the narrative. On occasion, it <u>is</u> the narrative.

What determines its placement is the effect the Letter will have on your message. If the Letter appears at the end of the narrative, it acts as a strong punctuation mark to your annual report, validating its content. If it begins on page two, it introduces the key message. If its message is critically important, the Letter might begin on page one. Like the narrative, the Letter can sometimes begin on the cover.

Consult Chapter 12 for more information on developing the CEO's Letter to Shareholders.

### Billboard Spreads

Annual reports readers don't like to face page after page of daunting text. So, it's a good idea to break yours up. In addition to the conventional text and image spreads of your narrative, consider inserting "billboard" spreads to vary the pace.

Billboard spreads mimic outdoor boards. Each combines a dominant visual with a headline and sparse or no text. Their purpose is to create a break in the narrative structure. Use billboard spreads to deliver key strategic messaging points, to spotlight specific achievements or events, segue to a new topic or move the annual report story along.

Be sure to include billboard spreads in your road map. Plan on having two or more billboard spreads; one by itself is confusing.

## At-a-Glance Section

This is a handy device for explaining how your company fits together. It uses a chart-like format. Columns represent different business segments. Rows represent many things: products, services, business markets, sales, and whatever else you want to throw in. There's no set length for an at-a-glance section; it can range from one to several spreads. Try to make it as concise as possible. Your annual report doesn't have to have an at-a-glance section. But be aware that analysts and shareholders like them.

## Directors and Senior Management

The Board of Directors page and Senior Management page usually occupy the last pages of the narrative section. They are sometimes found on a spread made up of the last page of the annual report and the inside back cover.

In most cases, the writer of the annual report is not responsible for the content on these pages. This is just a heads-up to include the pages in your roadmap.

## *Chapter Eleven*
# **Outlining Your Ideas**

Once you've nailed down the concept and roadmap for your annual report, your next step is to write a comprehensive copy outline. This isn't as dry as it sounds; you will be writing creative headlines and subheads as part of the process.

## Why Develop an Outline?

Creating a copy outline may sound like a tedious task, but it pays off substantially when you sit down to write the narrative copy. The outline is basically a list of bulleted copy points organized around the headlines, subheads, and bold text you plan to use on each page or spread. Creating those elements in the outline stage gives you a tremendous head start on writing your first draft. Not only that, it will give you more confidence in your writing.

In most instances, the copy outline acts as a pre-first draft. Whatever approval process it goes through, there will undoubtedly be changes made to it. But don't fret. It's much easier to deal with those changes in the outline stage—before you spend (read "waste") a lot of time writing the copy.

The copy outline reassures your annual report committee that you know and understand what the content requirements are. From the headlines and subheads you write, your outline also offers them a preview of your writing style. Again, if they have any objections, it's better to deal with them now, in the outline stage.

Once the powers that be approve your outline, it becomes your official blueprint for writing the annual report. Your narrative copy should follow it as closely as possible.

## Message Hierarchy

Breaking up the text elements on your spread makes it easier for readers to follow and digest your message. Many of your readers would be lost if you asked them to read an entire page of text set in a 10-point font. Why? They won't know where to look first. Nothing stands out. And there's nothing for them to skim. On top of that, the page will look too daunting.

What follows are the various text elements used in an annual report spread. There's no law that says you have to incorporate all of them, so just use the ones that serve your purpose.

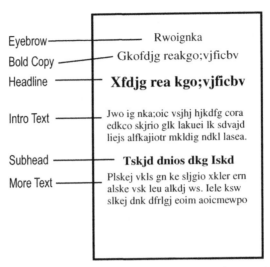

Figure 4: Message Hierarchy of elements on a typical annual report page

## Eyebrow or Heading:

This is a small heading placed in the upper left of the page or spread. It can be straightforward, like "The Plastics Division," or breezy, like "2008 in a nutshell." Its primary purpose is to orient the reader and provide some immediate context for the spread.

## Headline:

The headline has two roles: Its primary purpose is to pull the reader into the narrative. It does that by being interesting, compelling, intriguing, thoughtful, or smart. Its second purpose is to create, along with the bold copy and subheads, an annual report narrative that's more easily scanned. That means that if a reader only scans the headlines and subheads, he or she would come away with a good sense of what your annual report is about and what your key message is. (In reality, there are far more scanners than there are readers.)

Your headline can be any length. It doesn't have to be a complete sentence. I've seen some headlines that are three words long and others that take up three lines. So don't be hung up on construction—write the headline you think is best.

Style and creativity are important factors at this point. Your headline should not be too obscure, nor should it be too straightforward. It has to hit a delicate balance between the two. But most important, make sure your headline has a personality. Remember, it's not a title; it's a headline.

*Here are four sample headlines pulled from different annual reports:*

**We deliver knowledge 300 million consumers at a time.**
(Translation: We have 300 million records in our consumer database.)

**We don't ignore the realities of our industry—we make the most of them.**
(Translation: We don't over promise.)

**It started with an idea...and what an idea it turned out to be.**
(Translation: Look how far we've come.)

**We're keeping the development pipeline full.** (Translation: Our backlog of lucrative projects continues to grow.)

While it's not mandatory, try to create some consistency in your headline construction. Take the third example above, for instance. The headline is in two parts, separated by an ellipsis. The second part is a twist on the message expressed in the first part. Once you have a format, use it as the template for the headlines that follow.

**Here's a tip for headline block:** If you're having difficulty getting creative, write down in simple language what each headline is supposed to say (the translations in parentheses above). Then start playing around with the words, deleting some, adding some, rearranging them. Experiment with ways to say it more creatively. Another source of inspiration for your headlines is the library of annual reports you've accumulated. Flip through them. Sometimes, looking at headlines written by others can help guide your thinking. Between the two exercises, something will jell.

## Intro Copy and Bold Text:

Intro copy bridges the expanse between the front cover and the rest of your annual report. It appears on page one (the first text page), where it pays off the cover concept and introduces your key message. It becomes the filter through which the reader will experience the annual report. The point size of the intro copy is generally larger than that of the text. Often, the intro copy is bolded or italicized.

Bold copy is similar, but it appears on the individual spreads. In this context, bold copy creates a transition between the headline on each page or spread and the narrative text. It, too, is larger than the than the surrounding text, and often bolded or italicized. For consistency's sake, if you use bold copy on one spread, plan on writing it for all spreads. Strategically, both intro copy and bold copy help deliver your key message in concise form, making it easier for readers to understand. And scan.

## Intro Copy Example

*Front Cover:*
**Down the street...across town...around the world**

Intro Copy:
**At Any One Of Our 4,300 Local Offices, Each Day Brings A New Story. Whether It's Providing Hundreds Of Temporary Workers To A Large Global Corporation, Helping Small Business Owners Find One Permanent Employee, Enabling A Group Of Individuals To Transition Their Careers After Job Loss, Or Providing Employment Opportunities To People Who Cannot Find Them Elsewhere, Our Company Is There.**

## Bold Text Example

*Headline:*
**Managing the supply chain—end to end**

*Bold Text:*

**New aviation supply chain programs are on the rise—as is our share of the business.**

## Subheads:

Think of subheads as short headlines that subdivide the narrative text on the page or spread. They act like flags to catch the reader's attention. While your main headline represents the entire spread, subheads have a narrower point of view. They provide introductions to the topics on the page.

Subheads are a terrific transitioning device. They allow you to move from topic to topic without the need of lengthy segues. Subheads are also an essential layer on the message hierarchy, allowing readers to get a sense of the narrative text by simply scanning them.

Like headlines, subheads should have a personality. Here are four sample subheads pulled from actual annual reports:

### Expanding on a global scale
(Topic: International growth)

### 250 days and counting
(Topic: Safety record)

### Restructuring for results
(Topic: Becoming more competitive)

### Beyond point B
(Topic: Value-added logistics)

## Narrative copy:

The narrative copy, of course, is the primary substance of the annual report. Writing the narrative is covered in Chapter 13—Writing Style. But two important points bear mentioning here: Don't treat the narrative as a blow-by-blow recounting of the year and don't cram it full of content from every department or division in your company. If you do, you risk watering down the annual report's strategic value. You also risk losing readers, who don't want to wade through all of that information.

Rule 1 in annual reports: It's better to write too little than too much.

## Sidebar:

A sidebar is a story within a story. It's placed adjacent to the main narrative, either at the side or at the bottom, and delineated by a ruled box, different background color or both.

Use the sidebar to present interesting, relevant sidelights to your main narrative. For instance, a sidebar is an excellent vehicle for presenting customer stories, mini case studies, employee stories, a calendar of key events, or a story that is important to tell but does not fit into the flow of the main text.

Sidebars are part of the message hierarchy. Readers will often read or scan the sidebar rather than the narrative copy.

## Image Captions:

Use captions to describe the images, charts and tables in your annual report. Like sidebars, captions are part of the message hierarchy, which means they promote scanning.

Captions should be interesting. They should enhance the narrative text by providing new tidbits of information. Don't repeat what's already in the text nor overstate the obvious. For example, if you're presenting an image of a purple cow, don't have the caption read, "Look at the purple cow."

## Whitespace:

In graphic design, white space is the portion of the page left blank or empty. White space lets you ascribe more importance to your message. The more white space there is, the more the elements on your spread stand out. Be aware that the people on approval committees hate whitespace. They feel it is a waste of money. If they are paying for a full page, they want a full page—of text. So, expect some pushback in this area

## Formatting Your Outline:

There are many ways to construct a copy outline. Here's a format that I use. You can adopt it or create your own. Basically, you are sketching out the book in sentence fragments, numbers and bullet points.

**Front Cover:**

Your TITLE or cover line goes here

**Intro Page:**

Your INTRO COPY or reveal copy goes here. The intro is important. It helps set your annual report's tone and context. To give your approval committee a better sense of where your annual report will be going, it's best to write it upfront and include it in its entirety in the outline.

**First Spread or Page:**

Your HEADLINE goes here.

**Bold Copy:**

Your BOLD COPY goes here.

**Subheads and Copy Points**

Your SUBHEAD goes here.
COPY POINTS that support your subhead go here.
And here.
And here.
Etc.

Here is a brief excerpt from an actual annual report outline (starting at the subhead level):

A. (Subhead) PUTTING THE YEAR INTO CONTEXT
   1) 2005 was an uncertain time for the title insurance industry
   2) Compliance with the law not always followed
   3) Increased governmental and media scrutiny
   4) RESPA reform
   5) Costs of title insurance increasingly in the spotlight
   6) Lawsuits and fines are on the increase

## Now What?

Once you finish your copy outline, you're ready to begin writing the annual report. While you should stick to the outline as closely as possible, don't set it in stone. As you get into writing, you may find some of your copy points are better suited to other sections than the ones you originally assigned them to. Or a headline or subhead in your outline no longer makes sense. Don't worry. Your goal is to communicate as clearly as possible, which means you may add, subtract or reorganize your outline's content at any time if it will help the reader understand.

## Starting the Design Process:

By this time, your designer should be busy creating a layout for the annual report. A layout is a full-sized representation of what the annual report will look like, with dummy images and text in place. When you finish your outline, the designer will add your headlines and subheads to the dummy text in the layout. At the end of this step, it's ready to present to your annual report committee for approval.

## Chapter Twelve

# Letter to Shareholders

The Letter to Shareholders (also known as the Letter to Stakeholders, the Letter to Shareowners, the Letter to Owners, etc.) is probably the most important part of the annual report as far as readers are concerned. It is a direct communication from your company's CEO, and in some instances, the Chairman as well.

As the narrative writer, don't assume that you will be asked to write the Letter as well. Some CEOs prefer to have a hand in the writing themselves or else have someone closer to them in the company create a first draft. But let's say you are tapped to write the Letter. Here are the basic things you should know:

## Discovery

If at all possible, ask to interview the CEO as to the direction and content of his or her letter. Don't rely solely on the content you gathered during the initial discovery phase, even if that included an interview with the CEO. In a corporation, time changes everything, especially what's on the CEO's mind. If the CEO declines the interview, see if you can schedule one with another C-level executive. And, of course, prepare a new questionnaire. Here are some generic questions you may want to include:

What was your biggest challenge in (year)? How has the picture changed since then?

1) What were the most important events to (Company) in (year)? What was your biggest success for the year?
2) What new industry opportunities do you see on the horizon?
3) What are some of the ways (Company) is growing revenues? Earnings?
4) How would you describe the culture at (Company)?
5) What is the value of customer service at (Company)?
6) What is the value of R&D?
7) Where is (Company) headed?
8) If the reader could only remember one thing that you said in your letter, what should that be?

You'll also want to ask specific questions about major events and initiatives—whether they reflect good news or bad. Included in that list are reorganizations, acquisitions, plant closings, expansions, board retirements and the like. Look to the Director (or VP) of Investor Relations or the Director (or VP) of Corporate Communications for guidance on this.

### Organizing the Content

Redundancy is always a problem when gathering input for the Letter. The CEO will likely relate topics and achievements that you've already covered in the narrative. To use them in the Letter, you'll have to give them a new point of view.

What should the Letter contain? Here, again, turn to your annual reports library. Study the Letters; no two are alike. Make sure the letter has a subtle link to the annual report concept

Here are some generic buckets (sections) in which to put content:

- Introduction
- Financial performance for the year
- CEO's point of view on the industry
- How (Company) is positioned
- Expansion and growth
- Major achievements
- Building value for stakeholders
- Vision, strategy and future
- Thank you to shareholders, employees and customers

## Outline

Once you decide on the buckets, it's time to develop a another copy outline. As you did with the narrative, include both subheads and copy points in your outline.

Writing style is important here. Because the Letter carries the CEO's signature, it should adhere to his or her personality and writing style. That doesn't mean your subheads have to be straightforward. You can be a little creative as long as you don't stray too far from the CEO's comfort zone. Here are some examples of subheads taken from actual annual reports. You can easily guess what the topics were.

- *Doing What We Said We'd Do*
- *Starting a New Chapter*
- *Building Our Future—One Relationship at a Time*
- *The Myth of Market Size*
- *Where We Go From Here*

*Chapter Thirteen*

# Writing Style

Some of us learn to write as early as preschool, often before we learn how to add and subtract. Eventually, we find ourselves in Ms. Fromm's tenth grade English class, where we learn that the rules of grammar are sacrosanct. Then, in college, we hone our writing skills even more, learning how to express our thoughts in 15 words, when five would suffice. Then we get our first job, where we infuse our wordiness with all sorts of jargon and business-speak—to the point where we start to make no sense at all.

Why am I bringing this up? Because annual report writing is not the same as business writing, or at least, it shouldn't be. Annual report writing at its best is concise, fluid, conversational, and yes, even creative. This chapter is devoted to helping you achieve a measure of those qualities in your annual report writing.

# Rule 1: Less is More.

Contrary to prevailing wisdom, writing awkward-sounding, jargon-riddled compound sentences that run on for lines doesn't make you appear smarter. So what does? Writing more using fewer words. Don't kid yourself; that takes work.

Blaise Pascal (1623–62), 17th-century French philosopher and mathematician, once wrote to a friend. "I have made this letter longer than usual, only because I have not had time to make it shorter."

My wife's grandmother defined a "lady" as a woman who always studies herself in the mirror before she leaves the house and takes off one accessory. Make that a metaphor for your writing.

Don't write long introductions. In fact, don't write long anything. People just don't want to read it anymore, especially in an annual report.

If fourth quarter sales were off, for instance, don't waste a lot of words on the setup. It's better to talk about how your company is turning the situation around. The "Why" is always interesting, but it shouldn't get in the way of the real message, which is the "How"—what the company has put into place to change things.

Most important, be sure what you write makes sense. The following example, taken from an actual published Letter to Shareholders, does not make sense. The implication here is that along with writing less, you must also write with greater clarity. In this example, however, the words were already there. It's just a case of following grandmother's rule and pruning away the unnecessary ones.

**Before:**

"Our commitment to sustainability is deeply rooted in the culture of (Company). We believe it is our responsibility to focus on leveraging our leading global platform to bring together the best and most cost-effective, energy-saving and environmental practices from around the world to create value in a sustainable manner."

## After:

(Company) brings together the most cost-effective, energy-saving and environmental practices from around the world to create sustainable value for customers and stakeholders.

## Rule 2: Feel the Rhythm.

The first step to making your writing more fluid is recognizing that quality in the writing of others, whether it's an article in **Fortune** or a detective novel. Speaking of detective novels, here's the opening passage from Raymond Chandler's seminal work, the hard-boiled detective novel **The Big Sleep**. Can you sense the rhythm in his writing?

> "It was about eleven o'clock in the morning, mid October, with the sun not shining and a look of hard wet rain in the clearness of the foothills. I was wearing my powder-blue suit, with dark blue shirt, tie and display handkerchief, black brogues, black wool socks with dark blue clocks on them. I was neat, clean, shaved and sober, and I didn't care who knew it. I was everything the well-dressed private detective ought to be. I was calling on four million dollars…"

## Rule 3: Always Read Your Copy Aloud.

I can't stress reading aloud enough. If you only change one thing in the way you write, it should be this. All good writers follow this rule. It's the best way to determine how readable and fluid your writing is. It also helps you identify and change "speed bumps"—clunky words, phrases and punctuation that can hang the reader up and block the copy's flow. Of course, your co-workers, spouse or partner might think talking to your computer monitor is a bit bizarre, but what do they know? Go back and read the opening to **The Big Sleep** aloud. Did that make sensing the rhythm easier for you?

## Here's a snippet from an actual annual report. Read it aloud, just for practice.

"Living rooms, school rooms, hospital rooms—(Company) is bringing a world of communications to all three. Not just phones systems, but complete voice and data, high-speed fiber optic networks..."

I think of writing as a relay race. The baton is passed from the end of one sentence to the start of the next, carrying the reader along. Any word or phrase that stops that flow should be jettisoned.

There are things you can do to add movement to your work. Start by recognizing that good copy has a cadence. When you read aloud what you've written, do you hear the cadence of your words or do you just hear clunky sentences? If it's the latter, you probably have too many words or too many sentences. Or too many awkward buzz-phrases. Edit some out and read your copy again. Repeat as often as necessary.

## Rule 4: Exploit the Transitional Power of Conjunctions.

Conjunctions can help you add movement to your copy. They create smooth transitions between words, phrases, clauses, or complete sentences. In other words, they're great at passing the baton from one sentence or thought to the next.

There are all kinds of conjunctions. There are coordinate conjunctions, such as *and, but, or,* and the like. There are subordinate conjunctions, such as *until, although, while, even though, in order that, so that,* and *where*. And there are correlative conjunctions, such as *either...or* and *not only...but also.* There is also a long list of conjunctive adverbs you can use, including:

- Accordingly
- Afterwards
- Also
- Consequently
- However
- Indeed

- Likewise
- Moreover
- What's more
- Nevertheless
- Nonetheless
- Similarly
- So
- Still
- Naturally
- Therefore
- Additionally
- Besides
- Furthermore
- Likewise
- More
- Too
- Yet

Many idioms and other expressions can be pressed into service as conjunctions, including:

- As well
- To boot
- On top of that
- Not only that
- Even better
- Even so
- After all
- At length
- For example
- For instance
- In addition
- At the same time
- In any event
- In fact
- Not surprisingly

- On the contrary
- To be sure
- In the meantime
- Meanwhile
- On the other hand
- Equally important
- Just as important

Here are three examples of conjunctions in action:

1) Our Wisconsin mill has a near perfect safety record; even so, we feel there's room for improvement,
2) Employee morale is at an all time high—not surprisingly, so is our productivity,
3) (Company) is a global leader in water chestnuts. In fact, we're the official water chestnut purveyor to the White House.

## Rule 5: Use Punctuation to Create Movement.

Punctuation can help you create movement or emphasize points in your writing. The two most useful elements after the comma and period are the colon and the dash. Use the **colon** to set up or drama-tize the end thought of your sentence.

- At (Company), our focus is on a singular goal: meeting custom-ers' needs.

The **dash** can give your transition acceleration.
- Our signature Creole flavor is the unique taste attraction in every market we serve—from Maine to Bangkok.
- Some view specialty pharmacy and distribution as little more than getting the right drug to the right place—moving products from Point A to Point B.
- There are sixty different utensils in all—in stainless steel, nylon, wood and silicon.

As with salt, a light touch in using the colon or dash is preferable.

## Rule 6: Use the Power of Three.

A series of three words or phrases provides a good hook to engage readers. This type of construction is great for titles, headlines, tag lines and subheads. For example:

- Bank online—it's fast, convenient and free.

## Rule 7: Choose the Right Voice.

I believe you should write annual reports in a conversational voice. If your writing is too formal, you give stakeholders another reason not to read your narrative.

What is a conversational voice? It is a warm, friendly, everyday voice, not a stiff business voice or a sophisticated academic tone. A conversational voice is not full of compound sentences that are ten lines long. Instead, it contains shorter sentences, sentence fragments, dashes, verb clauses—anything and everything to add movement to the copy.

Remember, you're not writing to impress, but to inform.

Here are some examples:

- The wireless market is dynamic—driven by a never-ending search for the next cool thing, whether it's ringtones, games or handsets.
- Although our patients may have complex, chronic conditions that require expensive treatment, their needs are often basic ones. They may have a question about their insurance. They may want to talk to a nurse late at night. Or they may simply need a reminder that it's time for a refill.
- To appreciate (Company's) future, first look at our past. The company we were ten years ago, or even three years ago, is not the company we are today. We have grown in many ways. Our financial performance has strengthened enormously. Our global footprint has expanded. And our product/service mix is now far more diverse.

## Rule 8: Look for Disconnects.

Your copy should always have a logical flow. Guard against non-sequiturs—phrases or sentences that don't follow logically from the preceding text. Here's an example:

- At (Company), we focus on quality. In 2008, we earned four industry awards for our customer service.

This rule also applies to the relationship between your headline and body copy. Don't leave the headline dangling by itself; pay it off somewhere in the body copy.

For instance, if the headline of the spread is "The opportunity to grow," somewhere in the copy, there should be a line that talks about the company's growth. That seems obvious, but it's often overlooked.

## Rule 9: Keep Learning.

A bit of humility goes a long way in this business. This is to say, there's always more you can learn about writing. There are always new devices you can pick up from the writing of others, new sentence structures to try, new words to use. The moment you stop learning is the moment you stop improving. And that's disastrous for any writer.

## Rule 10: Embrace Change.

If you haven't guessed by now, becoming a good annual report writer involves changing the way you write. And like all change, that doesn't come easy. It requires an awareness of your limitations and a willingness to rethink how you write.

Writing annual reports is both art and science. Your task is to excel at both. Are you up to it?

## Chapter Fourteen

# Bits & Pieces

This is the miscellaneous section. It contains stuff left over from writing the other chapters. It's information that might come in handy on your annual report journey.

## The Madness of Committees

Like it or not, committees are part of the annual report process. Sometimes they give constructive advice, e.g., "We need to play up customer service more." Of course, they also give lots of frustrating direction, i.e., "I don't like the color green" or "You can't start a sentence with a conjunction or end with preposition."

When you present to your committee, try not to challenge them too overtly. Listen to what they say and go back and incorporate the good advice. Keep the color green if you feel strongly about it. When you represent, if they still object to the color green, change it. Another strategy is to bring two versions back, one green and one another color.

### Backpedaling

FYI: This is sort of like whistling in the dark. For example, you interview the product development team. They tell you that (Company's) widgets are better than anyone else's widgets. Great, you think. You develop a concept based on the superiority of (Company's) widgets. When you present the concept to the team, they say things like this, "Well, we didn't mean to mislead you, but we can't claim we're the market leader," or "Our competitor has just come out with a more advanced widget," or even "Our widget program has a ways to go before we can claim that."

Backpedaling happens. There's nothing you can do about it. Just be aware.

### No Negatives

FYI: Nine out of ten clients will object to using negative phrases in their annual report. Somewhere along the line, a teacher or their boss told them it was wrong. And the lesson stuck. So, if you put a negative headline or sentence in the layout, don't be surprised if they ask you to change it or rewrite it.

**Negative phrase:**

At (Company), our growth is not about to slow down.

**Positive phrase:**

At (Company), our growth continues to accelerate.

**Sentence Fragments**

"No sentence fragments." You'll hear that a lot. It's another area that clients often feel strongly about. But nothing beats a sentence fragment for punching up your message. Honest.

*(Blank page)*

# About the author

Robert Roth is an Atlanta-based freelance copywriter. For more than 20 years, he has written advertising and annual reports for some of the nation's leading corporations—including The Coca-Cola Company, Polo Ralph Lauren, Newell Rubbermaid, Neenah Paper, AGCO, Equifax, Progress Energy, Delta Airlines and Eastman Chemical.

robert@rothcopy.com

www.annualreportsolutions.com

Made in the USA
Middletown, DE
27 July 2022

70083708R00099